Eating What Grows Naturally

Other books by Kathlyn Gay

Meet Your Mayor & Meet Your Governor, 1967-68
Where The People Are: Cities And Their Future, 1969
The Germans Helped Build America, 1971
Proud Heritage On Parade, 1972
A Family Is For Living, 1972
Core English, 1972
Young America Basic Reading Series, 1972
Our Working World, 1973
Be A Smart Shopper, 1974
Body Talk, 1974
What's In A Name?, 1975
The River Flows Backward, with Ben E. Barnes, 1975
Look Mom! No Words!, 1977
Care And Share: Teenagers & Volunteerism, 1977
English For A Changing World, 1978-79
Get Hooked On Vegetables, with Martin & Marla Gay, 1978
Your Fight Has Just Begun, with Ben E. Barnes, 1980
Beginner's Guide To Better Boxing, with Ben E. Barnes, 1980
Boxes & More Boxes, 1981
Road Racing, with Douglas Gay, 1981
I Like English, 1981
Family Living, 1981

Eating What Grows Naturally

Martin & Kathlyn Gay

Illustrated by
Brian 'Woodie' Byrn

and books

South Bend, Indiana

EATING WHAT GROWS NATURALLY

Copyright © 1980 by Martin Gay & Kathlyn Gay

All rights reserved. No part of this book may be reproduced or transmitted in any form or by any means, electronic or mechanical, including photocopying, recording or by any information storage and retrieval system, without permission in writing from the publisher.

and books
702 South Michigan, South Bend, Indiana 46618

ISBN 0-89708-031-9
Library of Congress Catalog Card Number: 80-70278
First Edition   2 3 4 5 6 7 8 9
Printed in the United States of America

Additional copies available:
    the distributors
    702 South Michigan
    South Bend, IN 46618

Contents

	Preface	7
1	A Way Of Life	11
2	Just Plain Foods vs. Convenience/Polluted Foods	21
3	Who Becomes "One" and Why	33
4	Do You Buy "Natural," "Organic", "Health Food" or What?	43
5	Grow or Gather Some of Your Own Food	55
6	Eating Out	65
7	Mixing and Matching Foods	73
8	Dieting the Vegetarian Way	81
9	Fasting	89
10	Back to the Kitchen	101
11	Coping As A Vegetarian	113
12	Ernest Talk	125
	Books To Read	133

to Cathy
and for Art
who tolerates us across the table

PREFACE

They lived in a hollow on the side of the highest rise of ground which their clan controlled. The rock formation gave them little more than shade from the summer's baking rays and a dry spot where they could sleep during those wild nights of rain and wind. But Regrub and Aloc loved their home — even if they did have to share it with an ant colony and an occasional cockroach. At least it was better than living in a tree, although Regrub wished the distance along the path to the woods was shorter because it was there, at the edge of a stream, that she gathered berries and greens.

It was in this area, too, that she and the rest of our original "erectus" ancestors had swung from vines and had learned to survive. At one time the clan had been close enough to their food source to allow each member to forage for vegetation. But the move to the steppes brought with it a division of labor, and now it was primarily the females who made the run back to the green land to find the familiar herbs. Their return with armloads of food was greeted by the males and youngsters with shouts of delight and unceremonious lunging. This had gone on every day for many seasons, and all seemed satisfied that the pattern would continue. All but Regrub, that is. She became more and more weary of that daily trip to the stream.

So it came to pass that on one fateful morning, Regrub opened her eyes to the rising sun just like she had done every other day of her existence. But unlike all the previous days since she and Aloc had lived at the outcropping of rock, she refused to join the other females as they assembled to take the trail to the woods. They would leave without her, for she crawled over Aloc's still sleeping form to find a spot where she could lean back against cool sandstone and contemplate the real possibility of going without food this day. That worried her a little. Regrub enjoyed the berries and the feeling of fullness that came after eating the other vegetation which now seemed so far away.

While she sat and watched the sunlight illuminate more and more of her tiny home, her eyes happened upon a scene of much commotion near the ant mound which was set back into the farthest reaches of the cave. She leaned over to get a better look and saw about fifty of the little creatures swarming over the carcass of a particularly large cockroach. Struggling as they might, and acting as they do with one mind or purpose, the ants just could not get the roach in through the portal to their colony. Regrub had seen similar events, but never before was she so taken by the action of the ants.

She surveyed the drama for what seemed like hours, totally fascinated. It was then that the idea struck her. Perhaps it was due to her hunger. Maybe it was just the need for a change. Who can guess at the motivation of great innovators, even the cavewoman variety? Whatever the reasons, Regrub, primal person of our common ancestry, did something that day which none of her forebears or contemporaries had ever dared try. She reached out across the space separating her from the ant mound, plucked the large roach from her tiny house guests, and plopped the juicy black morsel onto the back of her tongue. Two chews and a swallow later, convenience food had been invented!

From then on, Regrub, one of the world's first vegetarians, could see no reason to gather berries and greens. It was too easy to satisfy her hunger pangs without stress and strain or even a thought about how to get her next meal. Certainly there was no concern for health or longer life. Those things would not even be labeled until eons later when people began to discover "natural" eating again.

the "Big" Tomato

chapter 1

1 A WAY OF LIFE

You've heard the admonition everywhere: "Get back to the basics of life." Environmental activists, who warn us of the costs of conventional energy production and the unseen hazards of nuclear power, urge us to use renewable resources and the sun. Educators are concerned about students who can't read or write and advocate getting back to the Three R's. People feel alienated from the political and economic decision-making processes and want to get communities back together again. Stress, the disease of the seventies, has almost become an epidemic today and people want to relax and tune in on themselves. Even our food supply can't be trusted and many of us are demanding more than the packaged, preserved and plasticized stuff on the market.

On the surface, it seems ludicrous to suggest that small fry like us can have an impact on the big fish who control our energy, educational system, and money supply and order our national priorities. The solution for problems in those areas are beyond the scope of this writing. However, positive societal change can come about when individuals wake up to realize the power they have when they are acting for their own best interests. Each of us does this when taking full responsibility for his or her life. The world is not everyone else's doing. The world is what we make it. If enough of us start making it right for ourselves, we may be able to get out of this decade without the apocalyptic crisis of too little consciousness meeting too big a need.

Food can be a starting point. The need for sustenance is as basic as you can get. And the answer to the critical question of how to control our own intake is to learn something about food and the alternatives to the mainstream way of eating. The responsibility you take for gaining control in this area will be a giant step if you have never given much thought to the effects of munching on that Big Mac. But there's no need to take a blind leap. In the next chapters, you'll find helpful hints, ideas, advice, and resources for further information on alternative eating. You should have some solid guidelines as you move into the world of vegetarianism and natural foods.

So, here is important point number one: *There is no such thing as a right way to eat.* That is, no expert can tell you what the best diet for your body/needs should be. During your childhood, your parents probably set the style or point of view for your personal eating habits. Maybe you are still following traditional patterns and wondering why you have a weight problem, or ulcers, or are just bothered by the fact that you've been eating dead animal carcasses. As a responsible adult, you should not have to cling to past experiences that have a negative effect on you. You can make the decisions about what you want to eat and how you want to live.

Maybe you are motivated to change your eating behavior because of personal appearance — for example, obesity, poor complexion, etc.; for health reasons such as hypoglycemia, hyperactivity, and/or constipation; for spiritual considerations (maybe you'd hate to be reincarnated as a piece of veal; or simply because you are curious about another way of life. Whatever the reasons for change, you should be the one to determine food patterns that are right for you.

Important point number two: *Success in this new venture will depend at least ninety percent on your attitude.* Friends, relatives, co-workers, and anyone else who is eating in the traditional style will look at the modifications you are making in your diet and tell you you're crazy or you'll be sick within a month, or are generally un-American because you won't eat Kentucky Fried Chicken, won't darken the door of Ponderosa, or eagerly delve into a bag of burgers and fries. Hang tough. Stay positive. In short order you'll have learned enough to reinforce the tremendous effort it's going to take to be different from the vast majority of eaters in this country.

Don't be shaken in your determination to step away from previous conditioning. Begin to trust your own senses and feelings about the input you bring to your life. Perhaps it would be easier to live the natural vegetarian life within the context of a society or a religion where whole foods and non-flesh eating are emphasized. However, the individual who lives within western junkdom can make strides toward more conscious living. There are enough people around today who have done it successfully, so you can learn from them and move ahead with confidence.

Important point number three: *While it's good to seek what one could call perfection in all areas of living, it's also important to realize that falling short of that goal is a fact*

16 / EATING WHAT GROWS NATURALLY

of life in this earthly existence we share. Keep responsibility a watchword. Monitor your attitude. Shoot for the moon and be happy with your effort.

Perhaps the experiences of Ernest will prove useful as you make your own decisions about the food you consume. Like most of us, Ernest has been raised within the tradition of convenience and taste. We could likely trace his ancestry back directly to Regrub and Aloc. Imagine how much conditioning has occured since their time. Actually you need not imagine; just watch a few TV commercials.

Indeed, Ernest counted himself among the members of the Pepsi Generation. That was eight years ago. Today, he eats natural foods almost exclusively and only an occasional piece of fish for his total flesh intake. But the transitions that have occured over the past eight years have not always been smooth. Being different in American society regardless of the belief in "individuality" is not an easy matter. Ernest's life during the seventies represented on a graph of food-eating habits would look like this:

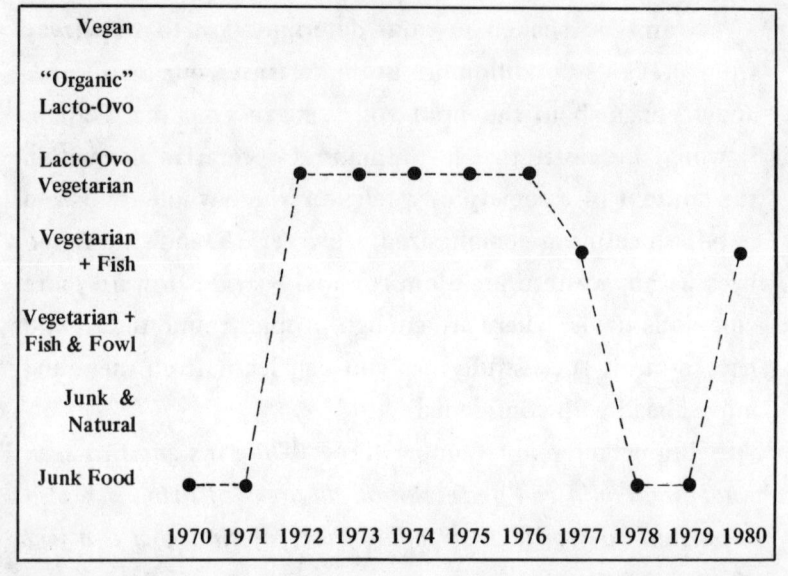

Category	1970	1971	1972	1973	1974	1975	1976	1977	1978	1979	1980
Vegan											
"Organic" Lacto-Ovo											
Lacto-Ovo Vegetarian			●	●	●	●	●				
Vegetarian + Fish									●		●
Vegetarian + Fish & Fowl											
Junk & Natural											
Junk Food	●	●							●	●	

At any point on that graph, if you asked Ernest about his food consumption, he would have convinced you that the choice being made was perfectly suitable for the time it was made. His attitude has always been the key factor in his changes. He knew the responsible party was himself and that's the way it always will be.

After twenty-one years of meat, potatoes, vegetables (grudgingly swallowed with no chewing and large gulps of milk) and sugary desserts, Ernest finally decided to make the personal decision about what went into his body. Had it not been for a friend's new-found dedication and zeal to revere all life and share these concerns with him, Ernest may never have questioned the habits his parents had laid on him. But he never could ignore the power of logical truth and his friend showed him how much sense it makes to take some care about what goes into this life factory we call a body.

He began to read books and take part in discussions on vegetarianism and natural living, and sample heretofore exotic dishes. He was soon convinced he had to eliminate flesh and synthesized, or fortified, or sugar-filled, or embalmed food. The task became a priority. And he took action.

One day he pulled everything out of his kitchen cupboards. Then armed with the minimal knowledge just gleaned from his friend and a few other sources, he judged each of the food items for its purity and life-giving properties. "Will this help me lead a healthier existence or am I eating this stuff out of habit or taste?" he asked himself.

Whatever failed this "test" was thrown or given away. Meat, sugar, white flour, instant brown rice containing three different preservatives, dyed cheeses, canned fruits and vegetables containing sugar or salt, soda pop, pasteurized milk products, iodized salt with a flow agent — these were just a few of the foods that became inedible for Ernest. He didn't know what he was going to replace those foods with, but he figured he'd learn quickly or be very very hungry.

Over the next few months, Ernest taught himself how to prepare natural foods such as whole grains, dried beans, yogurt, fresh vegetables and fruits, nuts and seeds. He learned to make the necessary substitutions for salt, sugar and the refined products he had become so used to and fond of as he was growing up. By the end of that first year, he was comfortable with his eating once more. He could cook gourmet vegetarian meals, he was happy avoiding fast food restaurants, he had lost twenty pounds of extra fat he had been carrying around since the days of junior high school, and he was feeling the power that the path of *eating consciously* brings to its followers.

Ernest continued on a lacto-ovo vegetarian diet (more about this term in the next chapter) for three more years. At times he was disappointed by his inability to find restaurants that catered to his dietary needs. This meant he stayed home a great deal of the time or went only to the homes of like-minded individuals for social dining occasions. There were moments when he was fanatical about what would or would not go into his system and he became overbearing as he tried to communicate this concern to his friends who ate in more traditional patterns. But overall, he was content to exist on the lower end of the food chain where no other creatures need die to insure his life. And what compulsive eater could pass up a diet that allowed him the distinct pleasure of eating as much as he wanted, whenever he wanted it, without gaining any weight from that consumption? Now that was heaven for a boy who had always been a chubbo! Vegetarianism suited Ernest well until. . .until it didn't.

Ernest went back to the meat-eating habit. In the wee hours one morning, after a night out, he went into a fast-food restaurant with a friend who ordered chili for both of them. Coffee and a hot fudge sundae made up the rest of the pre-dawn snack. Ernest hadn't had any of those goodies for over four years. The time was right to give them a try. He didn't really expect to survive the intake, but he thoroughly enjoyed the whole experience and his stomach didn't do any back-flips and his mind didn't play games with him. Not one guilty feeling or thought came to plague him.

Over the next few weeks, Ernest found himself functioning once more in the convenience eater's world of meat, sugar, and general junk. And while at first he kept telling himself it wasn't too smart to consume such trash, the ease with which he could obtain food like this fit in well with a life-style that he had recently developed. Not that he abandoned whole foods, fresh vegetables, etc. It was more like the pendulum swinging away from the fanaticism he had experienced in the years before. Now, he was willing to try previously banned foods, monitoring as he went along: "How does this sugar really affect me? What about chicken? Is there something positive for me in that prime rib?"

It was almost two years later that a concern for healthful living and the need to put some discipline back into his life made Ernest reconsider his eating habits again. For him food had always been the starting point for behavioral changes and he felt that a diet of revitalized food wasn't something he could be comfortable with. Flesh eating — especially that of cows and chickens — was beginning to bother him, not to mention the health problems of constipation and indigestion.

Also, it was no longer so simple to ignore the fact that sugary drinks and foods imparted quick energy but soon brought on lethargy and headache. And the final straw was the roll of fat around the middle.

Thus, Ernest made the decision to change once more to a natural vegetarian way of eating. This time, he drew the line by fasting (see Chapter 9). Through this sacrifice of food, he was able to gain the strength of resolve necessary for him to once more bring his diet into the realm of health consciousness. It was not like the first time. The absoluteness was missing. A cup of coffee at breakfast a few times a week, an occasional piece of pie, the touch of chicken gravy on mashed potatoes didn't contradict his basic fruit, vegetable, tofu, sea salt, honey, whole grain, miso, seaweed, distilled water existence.

Ernest isn't typical of vegetarians. Neither is he atypical. He's merely a person who is trying. In a world that scares us more and more with each new headline, the basic premise here is this: Those of us who try to bring control to our lives and our habits will actually find a sense of security in the effort.

Whether you do anything of the sort is totally your decision. The remaining chapters can help you pick and choose your way to a new mode of eating about which you can feel truly responsible.

Yet, a few words of caution. Take this and whatever you read with a grain of salt — make that sea salt, please! And keep your mind open. It's your own personal experience that will be the prime factor in any change. So trust yourself first.

1.

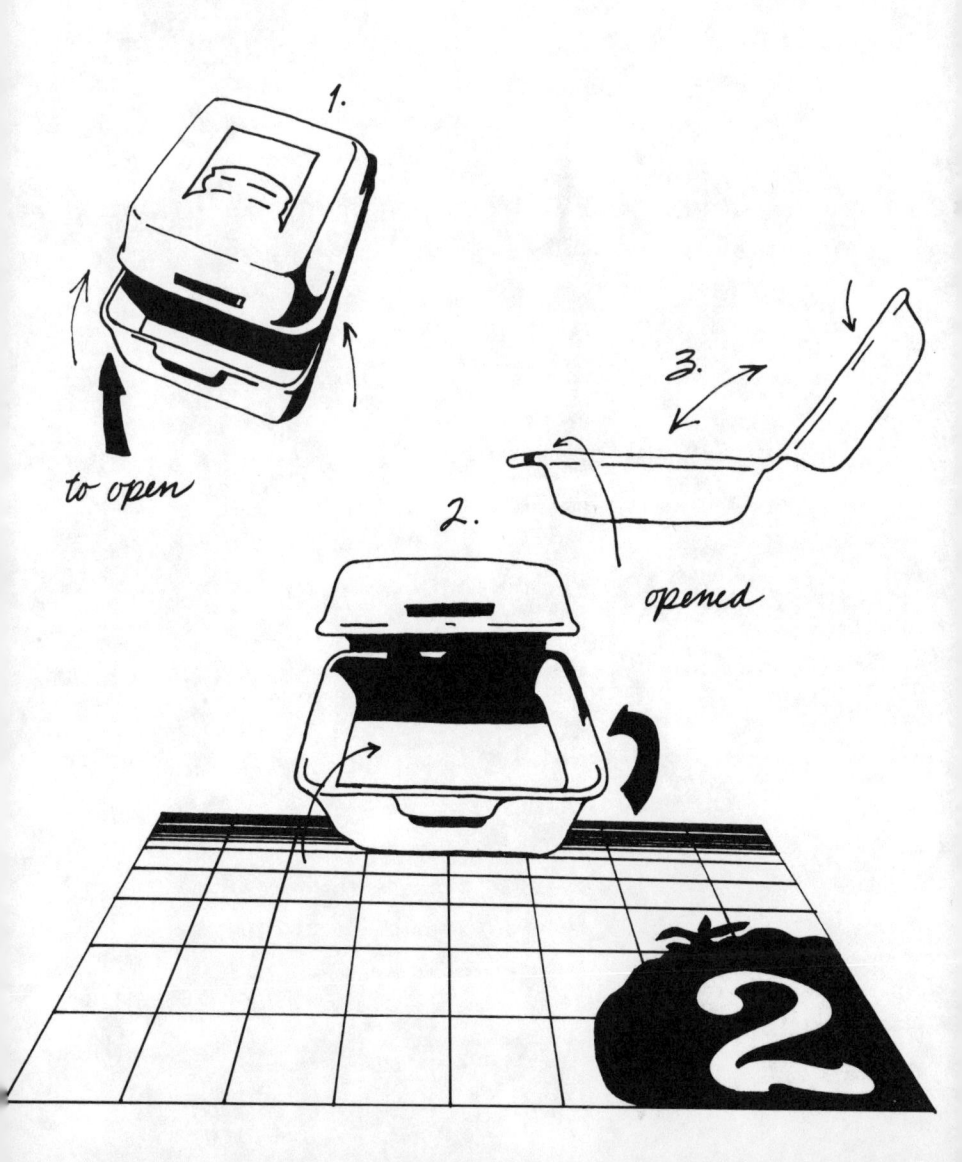

to open

2.

3.

opened

2 JUST PLAIN FOODS vs. CONVENIENCE / POLLUTED FOODS

When you become a responsible eater, you might begin to ask, as Beatrice Trum Hunter did in her book *Consumer Beware* (Bantam, 1972), "What has happened to the 40-ounce container, the average human stomach?"

It has become a target for corporate gain, that's what. Certainly we are being asked to buy the strangest assortment of tricked-up foods and hyped-to-high-heaven beverages in order for certain brand names to occupy space in our guts. Ms. Hunter states it well:

"...competition for those precious 40 ounces puts the consumer in the position of being a valuable pawn, with each eager competitor trying his best to fill the stomach with as much of his own merchandise as possible."

The food industry is huge and it wields incredible power and control. It and most other corporations spread their influence by educating us all as to the "proper" mode of living. Commercial television, radio and print media are at their beck and call, but the tube probably has the most pervasive effect. Since 90% of us have access to TV, imagine the power that is held in the grip of a few advertisers. They have incredible resources with which to study our reactions, trends, and habits. It's a simple matter then to make products that appeal to us. The appearance of products is now so important, and the public is now so conditioned that the right ad campaign could convince us to buy anything — from dog food to Presidents.

Can you envision an advertiser presenting the whole truth in that quick spot for, say, your favorite soda pop? "Yes, ladies and gentlemen, our Fatso Cola may lead to obesity, hypoglycemia, and tooth decay, but it sure does taste good! Your neighbors love it! Your kids will love it and love you for it! Don't be left out! Hop on the merry-go-round and buy, buy, buy!"

The large corporate food companies are big time hucksters. And judging by their end products, there is little social consciousness and even less concern about what goes into the preparation of various food items. Form is much more important than function. Convenience is the key word, whether in grocery packages or through fast food restaurants.

Perhaps convenience is wonderful in a world that seems to whirl faster each day. However, could it be that convenience and the hype that surrounds the concept of fast-fooding is actually a major contributor to the spinning we all have felt from time to time?

Slowing the corporate merry-go-round may be an impossible task, beyond that of a single person. If you get no closer to your food than the plastic clown who takes your drive-through burger order, it's not likely you'll be the one in control of your food intake. But you can step off that commercial go-round and onto the solid ground of personal choice. You have the absolute power to limit the influence of advertising, convenience claims, product acceptance, marketing plans and demographic studies — all of which are designed to show-and-tell how you should live your life.

This is most important in terms of tripping down the grocery aisles. Take a good look at what has happened to basic food. Mama would never recognize it from the lists of ingredients on packages. Oh, it might appear that you're getting the real thing. That's part of the scheme, remember? We are supposed to be convinced that looks and taste are more important than the real purpose of food — providing nourishment for our bodies. And of course processors know we'll pay a little more for the convenience of individual wrappers.

If the only reason behind the grab for this or that package is the convenience, appearance, and the taste that has been touted in a jingle you heard on the radio just before coming into the store, question that purchase. In the end you may buy it anyway, but gain the upper hand by learning a little about the stuff inside the familiar flashy container. Part of the important process of becoming truly responsible for your decisions regarding the food you eat is educating yourself. Don't just digest what the advertisers say about products. You're into *food*, not catchy phrases designed to snatch your dollars.

READ THE LABEL. Processed wood cellulose is used to increase the fiber content of some of the new "health" breads now on the market. Disodium guanylate is not a new Mexican food dish. Sucrose, dextrose, and corn syrup are all ways of saying sugar has been added. There may be a long list of synthetic ingredients and you'll probably need a glossary of terms (such as in *The Supermarket Handbook*) to know what each item is. At least the U.S. Food and Drug Administration requires that these ingredients be somewhere on the package. That's to our advantage if we take the time to check out the labels.

Suppose you are going to pick up a few "instant" foods for lunch. You zip along the grocery store aisles, selecting a package of chicken flavored soup, hot dogs, chocolate pudding, and a nondairy whipped topping. All of that will take only a few minutes to fix and it appears you'll have a substantial lunch with plenty of good, wholesome food. You can read the small print on the labels after you get home; you're in a hurry and don't want to take the time to puzzle over all that stuff that doesn't sound anything like food.

In the kitchen, your soup takes only ten seconds to reconstitute itself after you dump the contents of the foil pack into boiling water. Smells grand, doesn't it? Now, dig the wrapper out of the trash and read it while you're eating. Hmmm, this is interesting. You recognize food items like chicken and the vegetables and you can see tiny bits floating here and there on the surface of your soup. But who would have guessed there were so many other things in that small foil pack: Corn starch, hydrogenated vegetable oil, lactose, salt, natural flavors, freeze-dried chicken meat, chicken fat, monosodium glutamate,, sodium caseinate, dehydrated onion, sugar, dipotassium phosphate, mono and diglycerides, silicon dioxide, corn syrup solids, soy flour, sodium silicoaluminate, dehydrated parsley, dehydrated garlic, turmeric, tricalcium phosphate, spices, thiamine hydrochloride, lecithin, polysorbate 60, disodium inosinate and disodium guanylate, turmeric extract, lactic acid, and artificial color. Uh, well. . .maybe you'll pass on the soup today. Somehow it doesn't seem as "full-bodied" and "homestyle" as the package advertising claims.

How about the hot dog? Protein is good for you, right? Sure it is, but you might want to find another source of that nutrient, according to Michael F. Jacobson, a microbiologist, who wrote in *Eater's Digest* "A visit to [the] local frankfurter factory will cure most persons of their hot dog habit." Dr. Jacobson explained that his visit to a packinghouse "was a real eye-opener. The meat that went into hot dogs (and bologna) consisted entirely of fat trimmed from ham and chops; the only red meat was bits that were accidentally attached to large pieces of fat."

Dr. Jacobson also noted that dry milk or soy flour is added to increase the protein value slightly. Then the mixture is pulverized and emulsified before being packed into an artificially colored red casing. The cooking process then darkens the meat and it takes some color from the casing itself. Sodium nitrate and nitrite, sodium erythorbate, sodium ascorbate and sodium acid pyrophosphate are also activated in the cooking so that the frankfurter takes on the familiar color.

The role of nitrites as cancer-causing agents is still being debated. Recently the FDA refused to ban these additives because studies linking their use to the onset of the disease in animals were improperly done. However, Dr. William Lijinsky, who compiled extensive research on the problems of nitrites in foods, once told former FDA researcher, Jacqueline Verrett, Ph.D., that all test animals fed a combination of amines (which are found in many foods) and nitrites (found in cured and smoked meats) developed malignant tumors. The nitrites themselves may not be the carcinogenic culprits, but their combinations with other chemicals may cause reactions inside the human system that lead to cancer. In Lijinsky's opinion, "nitrites constitute our worst cancer problem." He, along with other researchers, have refused to eat foods to which the chemical has been added.

There is some question as to why nitrites are needed in cured meats. Processors cite the need to inhibit the growth of botulinum, the microorganism responsible for botulism poisoning. Yet, when pressed they will admit that it is primarily used to give meat its familiar color. After all, who would buy a hot dog that didn't look like a hot dog?

So, you're not so interested in the hot dog right now? The thought of one might cause a bit of queasiness. Anyway, you weren't that hungry. Maybe a small serving of pudding and topping will be just the thing for some quick energy. Flip off the lids and there you have it.

Over the teeth, past the gums, look out stomach, here it comes: water, sugar, vegetable fat, nonfat milk solids, starch, cocoa, sodium caseinate, dextrose, salt, artificial color, potassium sorbate, sodium stearoyl-2-lactylate, calcium carrageenan, polysorbate 60, sodium alginate, sorbitan monostearate, xanthan gum, guar gum, artificial flavor, sodium acid pyrophosphate, AND (don't forget there's topping, too) more water, hydrogenated coconut and palm kernel oils, sugar, corn syrup solids, sodium caseinate, dextrose, polysorbate 60, natural and artificial flavors, sorbitan monostearate, carrageenan, guar gum and artificial color. Belch!

What *are* all those things? Is any of it going to cause you to have cancer in a few years? Will you grow an extra arm or something? Who knows? Apparently no one is sure. More and more researchers are becoming concerned that the additives are there only to benefit the food industry, not the health of consumers. And there is real alarm over the incredible number of combinations of chemicals that can occur when a person eats a meal like the one just described. Soup, hotdog, pudding and topping seem innocuous, but the chemical mix of those foods might be downright dangerous.

Several years ago, Dr. Jean Mayer, well-known in the field of nutrition, noted that "we have many unnecessary additives... Their very number makes it increasingly difficult to identify potentially dangerous compounds."

Not all additives are bad, but neither are they all good. We need to be better informed about why and how they are used so that we can determine whether or not they should be in our food supply. The Food and Drug Administration is the watchdog agency of the federal government, responsible for judging what is safe for citizens to ingest. But the great quantities of additives that exist today (and the new ones that are continually being discovered) make this an almost impossible task. The FDA does require proof that a new chemical is safe for human consumption, but rarely delves into the accuracy of the studies or the type of research done.

Chemicals considered safe are placed on the FDA's GRAS list. Inclusion on this list of Generally Recognized As Safe compounds does not guarantee they are harmless to humans. Cyclamates and saccharin were on the list for years before animal studies determined they were carcinogens. Should we give over the responsibility for determining what is good/bad in our food supply to government regulators? Three studies — the Wilson Report, a Ralph Nader study group report, and a Kefauver report — have concluded that food companies receive favorable treatment over the interests of consumers. This fact, plus further research into the inadequacies of the FDA led Gene Marine and Judith Van Allen to point out in their book *Food Pollution* that "For some reason Americans seem constantly to have to relearn that the government's regulatory agencies belong to the men they're supposed to regulate."

When public reaction does mount, the corporate heads will do what is necessary to stem the tide of revolt. Here's a full page advertisement that appeared in a national magazine as a device to show that General Foods, one of America's food giants, is as benign and as helpful as any Big Brother:

"*Dear General Foods,*

What happens when I eat a preservative?"

"The same thing that happens when you eat any food — for example, an orange.

"Once eaten, an orange is broken down into the ingredients that make it up: chemicals. (One of these chemicals is — of all things — a preservative. It's called Citric Acid, and it's put there not by man but by nature.)

"The body then uses the chemicals it can, and eliminates those it can't. But the body doesn't choose between them based upon whether they have chemical-sounding or natural-sounding names. The body does care about two things: what the chemical is and how much of it is there.

"The U.S. Food and Drug Administration has established complex and thorough guidelines for the safe use of additives. . ."

There was more to the ad, but undoubtedly we are supposed to feel reassured just by reading this far. Of course, the implication is that anyone who would question the value of additives in our food is a bit stupid. And General Foods won't skip a beat in turning out more and more additive-laden products for us to buy. The motto: What's good for General Foods is good for Private America.

The fact is our food supply seems to be a combination of hype, sugar coating, and mush in milk. Food processors have become *manufacturers* of foods designed to appeal to all of our senses except common sense Such food manufacturers exist primarily to make a profit by using emulsifying, bleaching, buffering, and texturizing agents; sequestrants, stabilizers, preservatives, and antioxidants to approximate what food used to be. To fill America's tummies with the end products, it's hype the convenience, advertise the joy one can find by being part of the group that uses a name brand (Be A Pepper!), and generally saturate the collective consciousness with what it wants to hear: "Don't worry dear. Mother may not be there anymore with the homecooked meal, but we'll be down at the supermarket in that familiar package eager to take her place!"

a potato is a potato is a potato is a spud

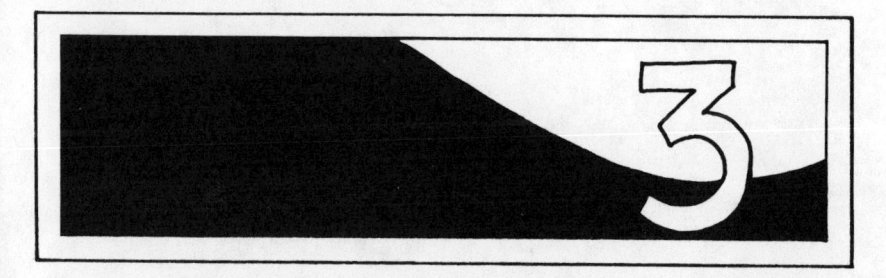

3

3 WHO BECOMES "ONE" AND WHY

Have you decided it is about time to change your eating habits? Do you believe such a change would be in your own best interest?

If you have a desire to try this new way of life – becoming a vegetarian – you'll probably want some type of working definition for the term. "Vegetarian" will be defined from here on out as a person who has eliminated flesh food from his or her diet. A *Natural Vegetarian* is one who eats foods as close to their natural state as is practical.

At the moment you may have the typical American eating habit – heavy on the meat, sugar, and processed, "plasticized," convenience foods. Some vegetarians feel that those who eat in this manner just happen to be somewhat lower on the scale of cosmic consciousness, but it is absurd to generalize like that. There is, as of this writing, no guarantee that your spot in heaven will be any fluffier because you abstain from eating meat. And we've all seen some pretty happy hamburger eaters and enough miserable carrot crunchers to know that it takes more than food to find peace on earth, let alone a reserved spot in the great beyond. After all, are some people doomed to a hellish after-life because their environment affords them little in the form of fruits and vegetables so that they have to rely on animal flesh for earthly survival? That hardly seems likely. At least it doesn't seem fair!

There is a wide range of eating habits in the world, and probably no country on earth offers more dietary possibilities than the United States. Think of the possible food habits as a continuum. If you place omnivorous folks (those who eat anything) on one end of the scale and herbivorous people (those who consume only plant products) on the other end, you can make a responsible choice, somewhere within that range. Gain enough knowledge, experience, and assertiveness and that will be an easy matter.

Most people who do look into their food habits tend to move away from the omnivorous/carnivorous group toward herbivores. This is especially true today with the weight of evidence beginning to pile up against the consumption of meat and refined foods with exotic additives. A lot more people are worried about getting cancer it seems than are worried about "salvation."

What are some choices within this scale? As one moves away from the omnivorous "American diet" toward the lower end of the food chain, an elimination process begins.

You might start by eliminating all chemical additives and sugar. Continue eating the meat and potatoes meals, but use only grain-fed (not hormone-fattened) cattle. Substitute honey or maple syrup for sugar. Use whole wheat products, not those made from white flour. In short, become a "natural meat eater."

Alicia and Ben did just that a couple of years ago. They raise their own cattle for slaughter, so they know what's going into the steak they're eating. Alicia will not buy a processed food product and you can't find a speck of sugar in the kitchen. While the couple feels that cattle equals food and their systems tolerate meat well, they have also begun to substitute nonmeat entrees for their usual fare several times per week. For them, this is a responsible choice because it is more a question of economics and availability. They have no intention of eating the overpriced, overfat, hormone-laced meat found now in most markets. They make sure that what they raise for their table will suffice.

Brenda's household has moved to change its eating in a different manner. She found that the meat-every-meal regimen was causing some body elimination problems for herself and her daughter. She decided red meat had to go. Now you won't find any old beef, lamb, or pork parts laying around in her refrigerator, but otherwise her kitchen would seem very traditional with Uncle Ben's converted white rice, Twinkies, Corn Flakes, sugar, etc. on the shelves. Fish and fowl stay in her diet, too.

"They don't act up as much," Brenda says. "Whenever I eat a steak, though, I just can't believe it. I suffer from either constipation or diarrhea. The taste of the meat just isn't worth it."

Lately, Brenda has even considered eliminating sugar from her household. Primarily she is concerned about her daughter's teeth since she has first-hand knowledge of what happens when you are a sugar junkie in your youth ("Look, ma! No teeth!") Brenda prides herself on being a good mother, so that is also beginning to mean taking a more responsible, albeit unpopular, stand against some of the agents in the diet which cause more harm than good.

You met Ernest in Chapter 1. He leans toward natural, whole foods and adds fish to his diet for variety and protein.

His friends, Bob and Carol, eat in a similar way. They chose to eliminate all meat and fowl, chemicals, and processed foods from their diet six years ago, based on a concern for health and ethical considerations — preserving animal life. They haven't regretted their move. The couple now has a two-year-old daughter, Amina, who seems to live on rice cakes with peanut butter, millet, and fresh fruits and vegetables. She and her parents are healthy and thriving.

Of course none of the people described so far fit the definition of "vegetarian" supplied earlier. While some of them do eat only natural foods, none have completely eliminated flesh. Bob and Carol keep a kitchen free of chemical additives and often go for weeks without consuming fish (which they consider much different from mammals or birds). However, they do not call themselves true vegetarians. Still, they don't get hung-up on labels. They just want to be right with themselves.

Marcy does that by functioning as a lacto-ovo vegetarian. Sounds rather technical, doesn't it? It's not. If you've had elementary Latin, you recognize that *lacto* is a prefix meaning "milk" and *ovo* is from the same language, meaning "egg." Marcy eats no flesh food (although she admits to eating commercially prepared tortillas and refried beans which almost always contain lard), but she consumes dairy products — milk and eggs — as part of her diet. This is the most "typical" vegetarian regimen in our society, and Marcy, like so many others who have recently moved away from carnivorous toward herbivorous habits, finds she can keep some of the more traditional dishes in her diet if she uses milk and eggs.

Marcy explains that when her consciousness about life was activated, she decided to stop consuming other living beings that had been killed for her nourishment. "It has been a good experience since then," she says. "Let's see, that was about a year ago. A good friend — a vegan himself — explained that he had had a spiritual awakening since doing away with the use of any and all animal products some ten years ago. I really don't know if that is to be my development. I'm open to it, but right now I'm comfortable eating milk products, eggs, and honey. And I'll continue to use leather shoes and books bound with glue made from hooves of horses — for now. My life has improved to such an extent over a year ago that I've got to be satisfied with my development. I don't want to stop developing, but it's nice to feel good about yourself for awhile. Being a vegetarian — lacto-ovo variety — has given me benefits on all levels of my life: spiritual, mental, and physical."

It should also be noted here that Marcy made the change over to vegetarian thinking/acting after she began operating a very traditional restaurant. Yes, she continues to serve ham with her eggs and she can still fry a sensational hamburger.

How does she justify serving the stuff if she won't eat it? One, she won't make the decision about what to eat for anyone but herself. This is a land of relatively free choices, she believes. Two, she has made a conscious effort to buy only the best products to serve, whether they be vegetable or meat. And three, there's a more than even chance her business would take a terrible beating if she told her regular breakfast customers she would no longer serve side orders of bacon.

Nobody ever said you have to suffer while you're getting your life together. Your changes can be made at your own pace. You don't have to jump from a junk food habit, for example, to becoming a "pure" vegan.

Not that it hasn't been done. Marcy's friend, Baron, was able to feel comfortable using zero animal products about a year after he decided to break away from traditional eating and earlier food conditioning. Accepting the tenents of *ahimsa,* Baron felt it was impossible for him to be an animal consumer in any form. Ahimsa refers to an eastern religious principal of doing the "least harm" to other living creatures. Striving toward this goal, Baron lives low on the food and product chain, eating only basic vegetable, fruit, seed, nut, and seaweed dishes, using no gelatin, honey, leather, soaps, buttons, glue or anything else made from animal byproducts. He believes this accomplishes the most good for him while doing the least harm to the other humans and animals with which he shares the planet.

The vegan, a true herbivore, is rare in American society. It takes total dedication to the effort of living with less when the rest of the world is telling you that you *need more*. Most vegetarians will never accomplish that feat. Yet, a good many keep that ideal in mind if not actually able to reach the goal.

Cathy, who owns a natural food market, has been a vegetarian for ten years. Just this past year, she has attempted to cut the use of eggs and milk products from her diet. She can see the benefits that some of her customers have derived from pressing toward the vegan ideal. As she moves away from being a lacto-ovo vegetarian, she believes she is continuing her effort to find perfection.

Yet, Cathy knows very well that other people may take quite different routes to "being right with self" and finding harmony with the universe. In her business she has been exposed to more food "trips" than most people could ever imagine. She has talked to *fruitarians* who, like the comedian and political satirist Dick Gregory, thrive on fruits, fruit juices, nuts and seeds. She has discussed the benefits of megavitamin therapy and watermelon fasting, colonic cleansing and mucusless diets, raw food regimens and zen macrobiotics. She has even met someone who claims to live by consuming only air — a *breathatarian*.

Which group or individual is on the right track? Nobody knows. The point is people can and do limit or eliminate meat consumption with various degrees of success. And many vegetarians in this country look to other societies in which people have lived healthy, vigorous and long lives without meat. In fact, the Hunzas of the Himalayas are often cited as an example of people who are free of disease, living on a diet consisting of basically goat's milk, yogurt, fresh vegetables, fresh fruits, whole grains, and on rare occasions a piece of goat's meat, served on feast days. Members of the group have lived to be over one hundred years old and the society's median age is much greater than that of meat-eating peoples'.

During both World Wars, there were drastic cuts in the meat supply in countries like Denmark and Norway. People lived primarily on diets of vegetables, milk, and some cereals. The grain that normally went to fatten animals for slaughter was used instead as a mainstay. Not only was this inefficient conversion of grain to meat protein ended, but there was a much lower mortality rate and fewer illnesses, according to medical researchers.

Studies were also made of Korean and American soldiers killed during the Korean War. The Koreans, who were basically vegetarians, were almost free of heart diseases, while Americans showed dramatic signs of arteriosclerosis attributed to the high content of meat and animal products in the diet.

A number of religious groups around the world limit or forbid their followers to eat animal flesh. In this country, the Seventh-day Adventists make vegetarianism a part of their teachings. While eliminating flesh foods from the diet is not a prerequisite for membership, the Adventists do emphasize the need to maintain the body as God's temple and recommend a vegetarian regimen, eating natural foods while in season, and avoiding highly refined foods like white sugar.

The U.S. Government has taken some steps to educate the country on the role of diet in a healthy life. A 1977 report of the Senate Select Committee on Nutrition and Human Needs did not suggest that we all become vegetarians. However, some of the recommendations included eating less red meat and high-cholesterol foods, but adding more poultry and fish to the diet. The Committee saw a need to reduce fat and sugar consumption and cut the daily average use of salt by one half, at the same time increase the intake of fruits, vegetables and whole grains. According to the report, such steps could help lower the risk of heart disease, bowel cancer, hypertension, gall bladder disease and cancer of the colon and breast while raising the vitamin and other nutrient levels in the diet at a cost effective rate.

The evidence for modifying this Americanized diet we thought we were stuck with is all around us. Seek out those who have moved along the continuum and hear their "true confessions." Read from any of the sources listed at the end of this book. Listen to the reactions of your own body. You may soon find a comfortable coexistence with your neighboring beings: animals or homosapiens.

JULY

Cauliflower

I once had an uncle
with a cauliflower ear
and a cauliflower nose.
...he hated carrots.

4.

4 DO YOU BUY "NATURAL," "ORGANIC," "HEALTH FOOD" OR WHAT?

Now that you're on the lookout for just plain foods that are nutritious, what should you select from the array of products on the supermarket shelves? Should you go to a "health food" store for some of your purchases? Do you have to prowl the countryside looking for a farmer who specializes in "organic" gardening? Is a "food coop" a good place to buy nutritious foods? What's a "nutrition center?"

There are no easy answers to these questions since many terms used to describe foods and markets for foods are often more confusing than they are informative. Take the word "natural" that's used on countless food labels these days and appears on advertisements for a great variety of food products. (It's even on manufactured items such as "natural" wood furniture and "natural" cotton clothing.)

When you're looking for truly natural foods, you'll be trying to find food in its most basic state. In other words, foods without artificial coloring, synthetic vitamins, preservatives, emulsifiers, flavor enhancers, texturizing agents, and so on and on. When a food is truly natural, very little has been added to the product to process or preserve it. Foods like brown rice, whole wheat flour, raw nuts and seeds, plain yogurt, fresh fruits and vegetables don't need additives to improve their quality or life-giving properties.

But watch out for the "natural" food products in the so-called "natural food" section of a supermarket or other type of food store. Some may well be whole foods in their natural state or foods processed without chemicals and artificial seasonings. Others may contain practically all synthetic items such as the ingredients found in most brands of ice cream, which you may assume are natural because processors are not required by federal law to list the ingredients on labels.

To make ice cream from whole products you would need only thick cream and real fruit for flavor, plus salt-packed ice for churning. But commercially prepared ice cream can have any number of more than sixty additives that are used to turn dairy products such as cheese whey or powdered milk into "creamy", non-crystallizing, "flavorful," colorful "ice cream" that is uniform in consistency. Some brands contain enough stabilizers and thickeners to keep the ice cream a solid mound or the consistency of bubble gum even after sitting at room temperature for several hours.

If you are in doubt about foods with the term "natural" on the packages, read the labels to see just what's in each product. A dry "shredded wheat" cereal, for example, says "100% natural whole wheat" "no sugar added," and that seems to be the case, according to the list of ingredients printed on the package. However, BHT is added "to help preserve the natural wheat flavor." Without the preservative, the product might be close to a natural food. Certainly it has more going for it than the dry cereals that are primarily sugar — some have a sugar content that's well over 50% of the packaged weight. Still, any of the whole grains that are in most dry cereals have been toasted, steamed, dried, or processed in some way so that few nutrients are left. Synthetic vitamins and minerals must be put back to convince consumers that the "fortified" product is as nutritious as any grains in their original state. (Don't be fooled — they aren't!)

Breads, too, may be labeled "all natural ingredients" or "no preservatives added" or carry some such catch phrase. Food processors are now trying to cash in on the public's growing demand for nutritious products.

Let's say you pick up a bread that has been advertised as having less calories but increased fiber. A number of medical experts are proclaiming the benefits of a high-fiber diet which tends to regulate the elimination process. Although fiber is great for most people, it's hard to imagine how eating sterilized wood pulp can be that beneficial! And that's exactly what one company has added to its bread — wood pulp — to increase the fiber content. What's wrong with keeping as much of the natural whole grain as possible in the bread flour?

You guessed it. That process might cost more, and as you are probably aware by now some food processors are out to fill your stomach and their pockets with very little thought about your health.

That brings us to "health food." Just what does that term include?

In the Health Foods section of a supermarket you are likely to find products for salt or sugar-free diets. Most of these foods contain chemical sweeteners or chemical substitutes for salt. Then there are meat analogs, products made from soy beans to look and taste like meat. A great number of these items are used by vegetarians who feel they must substitute meat-like vegetable products for flesh foods. Most are high in protein and other nutrients, but often contain a variety of chemical preservatives.

As a nod to "natural/health food freaks" (as vegetarians and other health conscious people are often stereotyped) you'll also find on the shelves a few high-priced whole-grain cereals and flours, pressed oils with no preservatives or other additives, herb teas, packaged nuts and seeds, and other pure food products. However, because of the location in the Health Foods section of the supermarket, these products are often priced higher than they would be if placed along with competing brands elsewhere in the store.

The point is, people who are marketing "health foods" are often trying to sell an image. They are promoting an idea of health to consumers who have little or no knowledge of how food and nutrition relate to health. In the average supermarket, you won't find a philosophy of eating for life. Instead, marketing and merchandising are based on what giant corporations view as profitable to eat.

The situation isn't much different in a health food chain store or so-called "nutrition centers." Just because the "healthy" adjectives are used doesn't mean you'll automatically find products that benefit you. Keep in mind, too, that health food stores often cater to consumers who want foods that fit into their particular health systems. These systems may have little or nothing to do with a natural vegetarian diet. Some people may simply be adding a high protein drink or a few vitamin supplements to their regular convenience meals.

So it boils down to the fact that "health foods" are those which have maximum nutritional value for your body needs. And most of those needed nutrients are in fresh, unprocessed plant foods – fruits, nuts, seeds, grains, vegetables – and dairy products as near their original state as possible.

If you think that was a round-about way to get to a definition of a term, try tracing the roots of "organic." Like the term "natural", "organic" has been used to develop an image that will sell everything from shampoo to frozen dinners.

Why should you, as a "new vegetarian" be concerned about what's organic? In the first place, the term has been abused by advertisers who want to associate any type of product with the image of naturalness and purity. Technically a product can be organic if it is derived from living matter or related to a chemical compound containing carbon. Accordingly, organic can apply to anything a person eats which was once living and/or is composed, at least in part, of carbon atoms.

For natural vegetarians there is another, more significant use of the term which describes the growing and processing of food. In that sense, organic means food has been produced with the use of naturally occuring fertilizers and no chemical pesticides. Crops are grown on soil that is conditioned with composted materials and mulch (layer of plant or animal waste). The fertilizers don't come from packages and spray bottles with oil company labels on them. They are in a more natural form and are composed of such ingredients as phosphate rock, granite dust, dolomite, wood ashes, blood meal, urea and steer manure.

Robert Rodale, Editor and Publisher of *Organic Gardening and Farming* Magazine, once explained that organic gardeners and farmers "wish to avoid the use of many pesticides that can cause damage to wildlife, and create toxic side effects...they also are very much concerned about the prevention of erosion, the adding of humus and other organic matter to soil to improve fertility, the preservation of small family farms, localized marketing of food, energy conservation, and proper nutrition. It is a rare organic grower who does not share those concerns, or pursue those activities."

Rodale's comments were supported by the late Dr. Robert van den Bosch, expert in the field of Biological Control at the University of California. Several years ago he noted that "Organic gardening and farming is a legitimate agricultural practice which not only yields high quality produce, but which is also energy conservative and makes efficient use of organic wastes."

Other experts have emphasized the fact that 'organic' when used to describe a specific growing method is an important designation for consumers who rely on the label to obtain foods grown without chemicals. And Robert Rodale has argued further that the term 'organic' clearly describes an alternative food system which allows "certain consumers the means to express political and social views through their purchases."

These same consumers also believe they have a right to buy organically produced food with a far superior taste than that grown by typical chemical production techniques. The taste argument might seem highly subjective — what one person finds delicious another might gag on in disgust — but you don't have to take these words as gospel. Make your own taste tests.

Try carrots for a starter. Compare the kind grown organically and those produced with chemicals. If your taste buds are alive you might pick up the metallic taste of chemicals used to grow the non-organic variety and you'll notice the sweeter taste of organically grown carrots.

Another test can be carried out with tomatoes. There's a real taste difference in tomatoes artificially produced and those grown under more natural conditions. For example, many tomatoes are harvested by machines while still green. Then they are chemically ripened with ethylene gas. The gas speeds up the ripening process, but there is less vitamin quality and an inferior taste, color, and firmness. Some consumer groups tried protesting this process, but the only solution offered by growers and agricultural specialists was to isolate the seventy chemicals that produce tomato flavor and reintroduce these into the product. Nobody would entertain the idea of trying to find better ways to grow, ship and merchandise the real thing — tomatoes which taste good naturally!

If you are able to buy organic foods, you'll have an added benefit. Your body won't have the extra burden of trying to eliminate toxic chemicals that may have been sprayed on foods grown by other methods. Organic foods are as free from human contaminants as is possible in this country. But beware! Don't fall for the term "organic" if it's merely an advertising gimmick. Be sure the term refers to the growing process for the food you are about to consume.

Now that you have an idea what natural, organic, healthy food is, you come to another problem. Where do you find the food that is going to fit that description? Actually you can start in almost any market buying fresh fruits and vegetables, although the produce is not likely to be organic. There just aren't many natural, organic markets in the country; most of those that do exist are on the west coast where sources are available year around.

If you shop in a supermarket take along *The Supermarket Handbook* by Nikki and David Goldbeck (a Signet paperback) which is full of advice on how to find whole foods. It also helps you identify synthetic food products which increasingly appear on shelves to replace top quality real or natural foods. Other helpful sourcebooks on food are the paperback editions of *Eat Your Heart Out* by Jim Hightower (Vintage Books, 1976) and *Food for People Not for Profit* edited by Catherine Lerza and Michael Jacobson (Ballantine Books, 1975).

In some parts of the country you can find natural food stores operated by communes or vegetarian markets near universities. The Seventh-day Adventist Church, long an advocate of healthful living and a vegetarian diet, operates six stores in different areas of the nation. One, the Pacific Union College Mercantile, is in Angwin, California and is a huge health oriented supermarket which offers a mail order program through Howell Mountain Distributors, its wholesale division. You can request a mail order catalogue by writing to College Market and Bakery, 15 Angwin Plaza, Box 249, Angwin, CA 94508.

Another excellent mail order service for natural foods is in Snyder County, Pennsylvania. Walnut Acres is one of the oldest and largest organic farms in the country. According to *The Last Whole Earth Catalog* (and the personal experiences of the authors of this book), Walnut Acres is one of the most reputable sources in the U.S. for organic foods. More than 35,000 customers probably agree because they pay mailing costs on top of the regular prices for products. If you want to check out their organically grown produce, canned goods, grains, baked items and dairy products, write for their listings at Walnut Acres, Penns Creek, PA 17862.

The *Guide to Organic Food Shopping and Organic Living* is another mail order source. It's available from Rodale Press, 33 E. Minor Street, Emmaus, PA 18049 or you might find it as a reference in your public library.

To have a whole food source nearby, you might consider joining a cooperative buying club or starting one of your own. There are a number of books and pamphlets on how to establish a food coop. One good source is *Food Coops* by William Ronco (Beacon Press, 1974). Also, check with people who operate vegetarian restaurants or natural food markets; they may be able to help with information on how to get in touch with a coop or get one underway.

Don't forget roadside stands in the country. You might be able to buy organic produce. Talk to farmers in your area and ask about the availability of fresh fruits and vegetables. Also inquire about milk from grain or grass fed cows and eggs from free-roaming chickens (rather than eggs produced by robot-like chickens that are always kept in cages).

For most natural vegetarians, the job of finding good food is tough, but don't give up if you run into roadblocks. You'll have to develop some new skills and learn new ways of doing things. Even if you live in a year-around growing climate, you'll want to learn how to cook grains that are non-instant, make your own yogurt and peanut butter, and combine foods for complete protein.

If you get discouraged, turn to vegetarian friends for help or such handbooks as *Laurel's Kitchen* by Laurel Robertson, Carol Flinders, and Bronwen Godfrey which has excellent sections on how to get started as a vegetarian. (A paperback edition of the handbook has been published by Bantam.) You'll find good ideas for food sources in the cookbooks listed in Chapter 10, and in the bibliography.

Finally, you might want to try growing some of your own food, as suggested in the next chapter. It's really satisfying when your crops start to bear and you can eat what you have produced. You might even can or freeze surplus fruits and vegetables to assure a better food supply. Right now, though, you can see if you are interested in testing out your green thumb.

radish 1 radish 2 radish 3 radish 4

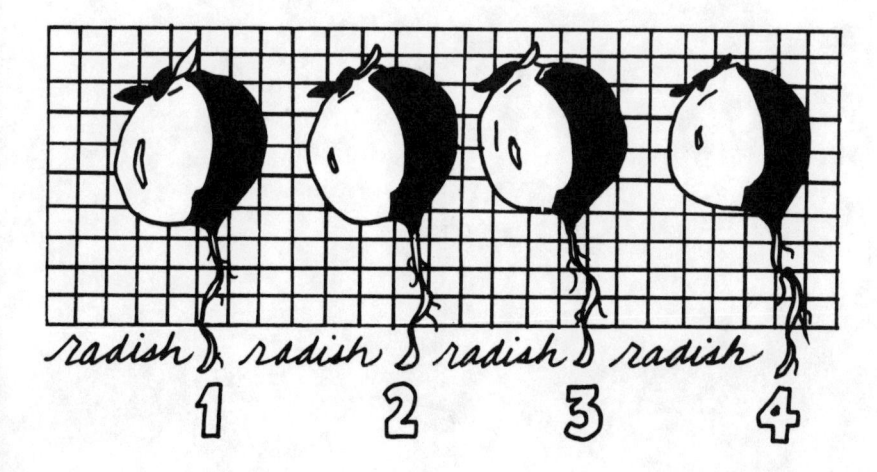

chapter 5

5 GROW OR GATHER SOME OF YOUR OWN FOOD

If you have never turned a shovelful of dirt or even watered a house plant, gardening may seem like a lot of work. What about planting knowledge and preparing the soil? You might also be concerned about finding a plot of ground and the cost of tools. Isn't it difficult to grow nutritious foods?

The answer is no, if you take things one step at a time and remember that you don't have to grow all of your food unless you want to. If you produce just a few edible crops, you'll save not only money but you'll also be sure of organic growing conditions.

One of the most simple and inexpensive gardens can be started in your own home by growing sprouts and greens. Use alfalfa, sunflower seeds, mung beans, wheat, soybeans, chickpeas, celery seed or radish seeds, to mention a few possibilities.

Seeds and grains could be eaten as they are, but they are not particularly desirable as food unless you cook them. They have a high starch content which makes them hard to digest. Once seeds and grains sprout, though, they convert to simple sugars and amino acids (proteins broken down). As crisp vegetables, they are rich in vitamins and minerals and easily assimilated by the body. Sprouts are great in salads and on sandwiches; they can be cooked with vegetables, sauteed in a little butter, or blended with drinks. Most vegetarian cookbooks or organic gardening books include information on sprouts and how to grow as well as prepare them. But here a few suggestions for starters:

Pour about a quarter to half a cupful of seeds in a wide-mouthed jar and cover with water. Use about two parts water to one part seeds and soak them overnight in a warm (about 70 degrees) dark place such as a closet, pantry, or cupboard. Make a sieve for draining by covering the mouth of the jar with cheesecloth or piece of clean nylon stocking. Secure with a rubber band or string.

Drain the soaking liquid from the seeds the next morning. Most health-conscious folks save the soaking liquid, which is high in nutrients, to use in soups or to water house plants. Return the jar to a warm dark place, but remember to rinse the seeds with lukewarm water two or three times during the day. Drain well after each rinsing.

Follow the rinsing procedure for about three days and your sprouts will be ready for "harvest." Some sprouts, such as those from soybeans, may take about five days.

If you want your sprouts to form chlorophyl, place them in direct sunlight long enough to give them a green color.

You can also grow greens or sprouts indoors by planting seeds and grains in a flat tray or shallow box or pan. Soak the grains or seeds overnight. Then spread them on a dark, porous soil. Ask someone in a garden shop to help you with this or buy some peat moss and mix it with your garden soil. Then moisten the soil and seeds without soaking them.

Cover with a damp cloth, plastic sheet or about 1/8 inch of soil. Again, the "garden" should be damp, but not wet. Store in a dark, warm place. After three days, place in the sunlight for growth. In another three or four days, you'll have green grasses for salads or for blending and juicing.

If you want to take sprouts along on a trip (or just prefer portable containers), use pint size plastic containers such as the empties from delicatessen foods or ice cream. Prepare them for drainage by heating the tines of a fork over a gas burner. Be sure to use a potholder on the fork handle to protect yourself from burns. When the tines are red hot, insert them into the bottom of the container. Repeat the process until the bottom is covered with small holes. Be careful not to make the holes too large or some seeds, like alfalfa, will fall right through. Let the fork just break into the plastic so that water can drain out. An ice pick will do the job very well too.

Next, place the container with the holes inside an identical one without holes. This way you can catch the excess water after rinsing. Put the plastic lid on top. This allows plenty of light to come in so chlorophyl growth will not be hampered. These sprouters are excellent when you want to grow only small quantities.

Along with sprouts, you can grow a variety of common garden vegetables indoors. Duane Newcomb, an expert on intensive gardening, has written two helpful books on the subject: *The Postage Stamp Garden Book* and *The Apartment Farmer*. In both, you'll find glossaries, ideas on preparing garden beds, planting charts for when and how to plant, lists of seed companies and instructions on how to make compost from kitchen waste. In *The Apartment Farmer* there are instructions for using everything from an old coffee pot to a whiskey barrel as planters. If you've never thought you could grow a thing, you'll have a good chance for success by following the directions in these two publications.

Don't forget mass circulation magazines for advice. They often have articles about gardening with information about plotting out whatever space is available, recommendations on which vegetables should be planted in sunny areas and how to prepare soil, start seeds indoors, water plants, fertilize, weed and keep your garden growing. Your public library, local book store, or garden shop should have many resources also.

To find published materials on natural, organic gardening, check *The Last Whole Earth Catalog*, which has an annotated list on the subject. One of the best sources for instructions on organic growing comes from Rodale Press, Emmaus, Pennsylvania 18049, which publishes such titles as *Step-by-Step to Organic Vegetable Growing; Best Ideas for Organic Vegetable Growing; The Organic Way to Plant Protection* and *The Ruth Stout No-Work Garden Book.*

Rodale also publishes *Organic Gardening and Farming,* a monthly magazine that carries a broad spectrum of articles dealing with organic foods, from planting to preparing the final products. One recent feature explained how to grow gardens away from home, in plots that might be outside the city limits. Another told how to grow mushrooms. You can get information on pest control, making compost for enriching your garden, and producing natural maple syrup, plus many other subjects.

Rodale's *Encyclopedia of Organic Gardening* is the "bible" for organic growing. It defines what that type of farming system is all about and also includes interesting reading on herbs and herb culture, plus descriptions of different varieties. Such information is a great help as you get into more and more natural cooking and growing. You can supplement your food supply by gathering herbs and wild foods.

Wild plant life is a subject covered in a number of recent publications. Darcy Williamson published a resource book in 1980 on *How to Prepare Common Wild Foods*, which you may be able to find in your local bookstore or order it from Darcy Williamson, Box 1032, McCall, Idaho 83638. A lot of the recipes for baked goods and sauces contain ingredients which are not whole foods, but you can make substitutions, using honey, whole wheat flour and butter rather than sugar, white flour and margarine as suggested.

The Williamson book describes and illustrates dozens of herbs and wild plant life so that you can recognize them along the roadside, in wooded areas, streams, and meadows. Wild apples, blue elderberries, cattails, common dandelions, miner's lettuce, wild mint, mushrooms, wild onions, and watercress are just a few of the foods covered.

Another good source of information on this subject is *Common & Uncommon Uses of Herbs for Healthful Living* by Richard Lucas. (Arco Publishing, Inc., 219 Park Avenue South, New York 10003.) This paperback emphasizes the healing nature of herbs but also describes various properties of the plants along with accounts of how they've been used over the centuries.

You may be lucky enough to find a class on edible wild foods. A number of environmental centers, park districts and schools are offering courses on the subject. One such course in south suburban Chicago is conducted by Cindy

Squires who works with five school districts to show kids they don't have to be limited to the cultivated plants they normally think of and prepare as food. However, Cindy cautions kids and adults that they can't go out and just pick or gather any growing thing. She particularly stresses the importance of knowing which mushrooms are edible and how to identify poisonous varieties.

According to Ms. Squires, some of the wild foods that might be found in your own backyard, so to speak, include milkweed, cattails, pepper grass, wild grape leaves, shepherd's purse, and mushrooms. Squires says "you can batter fry all of them." If you are wondering about taste, particularly of a plant like cattails, she reports that the brown fuzzy part (which is fixed like corn on the cob) is somewhat like beans in flavor.

You can use a number of different varieties of wild mint leaves for flavoring and the plants, if given a start, will grow easily in your own yard. So will dandelions and blue violets, wild plants that are highly nutritious.

Whether growing your own vegetables or gathering wild plants, you can eliminate the chemical pesticides that are sprayed on most fruits and vegetables grown for retail markets. This can be a real health benefit if you take any stock at all in a September 1980 Los Angeles Times report on the risks of pesticide residues on foods. In a three-part series of articles based on a year-long investigation, staff writer Ronald B. Taylor presented findings that included these unsettling facts:

— American farmers use nearly 300 different types of poisons to control weeds and pests and to produce greater crops of unblemished fruits and vegetables.

— Laboratory tests have shown that there can be a dozen or more different chemical residues on, say, one head of lettuce or box of strawberries. Very little is known about the effect of multiple pesticide residues, but a number of individual pesticides have been tested on laboratory animals, causing cancer, nerve damage or birth defects.

— Federal agencies are supposed to determine the amounts of poisons on food that can be safely tolerated by consumers, but some scientists insist there is no such thing as a "safe" tolerance level for a carcinogen.

— There are only a few government inspectors to check the billions of pounds of produce going through wholesale markets to retail outlets each year, and if contaminated fruits and vegetables are found it takes so long for test results that much of the food has already been consumed.

The lengthy report clearly indicates that the government (both at the state and federal levels) is willing to take a calculated risk that some consumers may get cancer. In addition, the report states: "American consumers have grown accustomed to huge selections of fresh produce in recent years, and although some people argue that it is the heavy use of pesticides that has helped make this possible, others insist that crop poisons are often used to improve the looks of produce rather than to increase production."

On that pessimistic note, you may decide that growing your own food is not such a hassle after all. If you do have to buy all of your produce from a market, at least give everything a good bath and pray that an FDA official is right when he said recently "The public is well-protected. The amount of pesticide residues coming through is inconsequential."

Lettuce

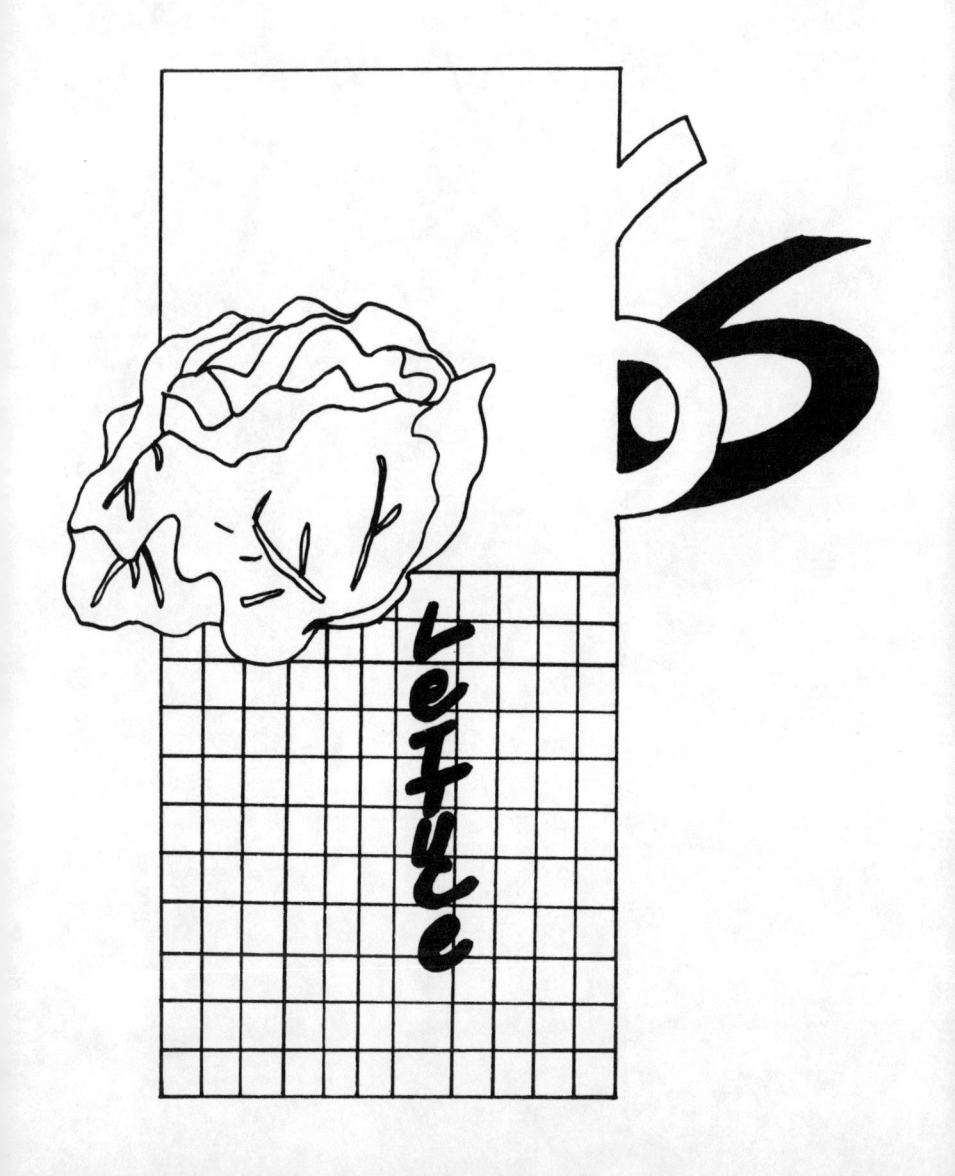

6 EATING OUT

If you want to go out for a meal, how would you as a vegetarian find a restaurant that serves "your kind of food"? Suppose you're traveling. What kinds of food/restaurants are available for vegetarians on the move? What about invitations to dinner or an evening out with meat-eaters? Do you decline or is there a way to get by at a non-vegetarian meal?

Eating out can pose a variety of problems, but there are a number of ways to manage and enjoy another's cooking as well. First, be sure to check out your own community. There might be a vegetarian restaurant in a mall or shopping center or refurbished store front in an older section of town. Often vegetarian restaurants flourish near college campuses. Look in the yellow pages of the phone book for ads showing locations.

If a vegetarian restaurant isn't listed, call a natural/health food store and ask about eating places. You might get a good lead. That's also a good technique to use while traveling. You may be surprised at the number of natural food or vegetarian eateries around. They have been popping up all over the country for the past few years. *The Vegetarian*

Times Guide to Dining Out in the U.S.A. (Atheneum, 1980) lists more than 500 restaurants and is a valuable reference while on the road.

Maybe you prefer to carry your own food en route, especially on a camping trip. Depending on how long you travel and your individual taste, you might take along alfalfa, mung bean, wheat, lentil, or soybean sprouts. Any of these can be easily grown in a car or camper.

If you have cooking facilities, grains such as oats, millet, barley, bulghur wheat, rice, wheat flakes, rye flakes make a simple and substantial meal. You can cook up grains for a breakfast cereal, adding milk and honey, or yogurt and maple syrup, or kefir and date sugar. Or make a main dish for lunch or dinner with a little butter and tamari soy sauce or other seasonings.

You can prepare bulghur wheat ahead of time to have on hand while you're traveling. Mix two parts bulghur with one part warm water in a container that you can cover tightly. If you're going by car, put the container on a sunny ledge by your rear window, or anywhere that it will stay warm. In about an hour, the grain will be fluffy and ready to use when you stop. It's excellent in a tabouli salad (See Chapter 10.)

Don't forget eggs if you are into eating them. They're great protein and energy food, and easy to carry in an ice chest. Put in some milk, cheese, yogurt or kefir, too.

Buy fresh produce where you find it along the way. Take advantage of those roadside stands. The food will probably be fresher than what you get at home and it might even be less expensive. And if you've read up on wild plant life, you'll be able to gather some "free food" along the way.

Nuts and seeds are great for fill-ins. You won't need large quantities at any one meal, so a couple of pounds should be plenty for a week or two on the road. Trail mix is a great traveling snack, too.

While on a trip or just out for the day, you may find on occasion that you have to eat in a "regular" restaurant. Then what? You'll soon learn to *ask* for what you want. It's fairly simple to get a meatless meal in almost any restaurant by ordering side dishes or ala carte items from the menu. Or just order the specialty of the house sans meat. But it's another thing to get "just plain foods" or whole foods prepared without sauces or gravies containing ingredients you may not want to ingest.

Some fairly "safe" items include fresh vegetable dishes (ask if they are prepared from fresh produce or from the can or frozen food packages), and fresh fruit plates with or without cottage cheese (again, ask if the fruit is from the can; to some people "fresh" means a can has just been opened or that bowls or salad plates of canned fruit have been prepared that day).

A number of restaurants are now serving vegetarian entrees so you can check them out, too. There could be a vegetarian quiche or pizza on the menu. Sometimes there are vegetable soups but you'll have to ask if they're made from "pure" vegetable stock or a meat base.

As many vegetarians have discovered, you can even eat in a fast food joint — if you get desperate. Most of the franchise places have a salad bar with fresh produce or you can get orders of cole slaw, potato salad or maybe a baked potato.

Making food decisions in a restaurant allows a little more freedom of choice than when you are invited to homes of friends or relatives to dine. How do you handle those social occasions that revolve around food? Well it's pretty safe to bet that as a vegetarian you'd be miserable at a party where the buffet table is loaded with platters of meat-filled hors d'oeuvres, unless you learn how to nibble around the fillings or eat the decorative lettuce and parsley. Of course with the increasing number of people watching their weight, you might find the buffet includes fresh vegetables with dips and possibly some cheeses. Then you're in luck.

For a sit-down dinner with meat as the main course, there can be a real dilemma. If you eat your vegetables and leave the meat, you're liable to insult the cook. And seldom can anyone who has prepared a fancy sugary dessert understand why you would turn it down, particularly when you're not "on a diet" for weight loss. The best solution, in some cases, might be to turn down invitations which would cause discomfort all around. Simply let people know you seldom eat out because of diet "restrictions" but another type of social get-together would be fine. Eventually you may gravitate toward gatherings in which vegetarians meet to eat and gain a whole new circle of friends or acquaintances.

One beneficial aspect of sociable eating is the manner in which food is eaten. Often there's a relaxed atmosphere. The tensions and problems of the day can be put aside, and people are inclined to eat more slowly.

The way a person eats can be almost as important as the food consumed. It does little good to devour a meal with gobbles and gulps on the gallop, as many nutritionists and health experts have pointed out.

Hans Holzer, in his book about *The Vegetarian Way of Life* notes that ". . .ideally vegetarians do not rush their meals, but allow their bodies to be in a fully relaxed state prior to eating or drinking." Of course this isn't always possible, but a few relaxing exercises before meals, such as deep breathing, simple bending calisthenics or various yoga positions, can help.

"Even more important than the physical state before eating is the mental state of the individual," Holzer writes. "Mind controls body, mind triggers bodily reactions. To come to the table with one's mind filled with problems, with worries, with unresolved conflicts, is to invite trouble."

It follows that a state of serenity is a good rule for digesting food properly. Many natural foods and vegetarian restaurants encourage a relaxed state while eating. The nationally known Ranch House in Ojai, California attracts people from all over southern California and many parts of the nation because of its gracious un-hurried way of dining in a garden setting.

Alan Hooker, who founded the gourmet restaurant and has created hundreds of recipes, which are compiled in several cookbooks, says that his whole philosophy is based on a "sensitive approach to food and eating." Dinners are prepared to order just twice in the evening and by reservation only, then placed on the table by hostesses who attempt to establish positive relationships with diners.

The Ranch House serves some meat dishes, as well as total vegetarian meals, but Mr. Hooker, a natural vegetarian himself, feels that the most essential part of preparing meals is to have absolutely fresh produce. The organic fruits and vegetables come from farmers or ranchers in the area, some of whom grow only one or two crops like artichokes or zucchini squash or limes. The cooks at the Ranch House use natural herbs from the gardens which surround the patio area where meals are served.

Prices are high at the Ranch House, because of the highly individualized service, but some more moderately priced vegetarian or natural foods restaurants also promote a peaceful relaxed atmosphere. Even small lunch counters make use of patios, garden settings, or if meals must be served indoors, plant life is used in many restaurants to simulate the natural habitat which has a calming effect on customers. Some proprietors encourage meditation and wall hangings with philosophical sayings may help create a tranquil mind for mealtime.

No matter where you "break bread" with others, try not to overdo it. Usually birthdays, holidays and other special occasions call for get-togethers with lots of food and drink. Americans generally have a lot of food available, so the tendency is to let the feast become the total experience. Don't eat to the point of gluttony. Rather, let food play a complimentary role in sharing friendships, happiness, or in establishing positive relationships.

One of the most personalized ways vegetarians eat out is at an old fashioned carry-in or potluck. You can prepare a favorite dish to share as an extension of yourself just as you will sample the offerings of others.

Once again, though, simplicity is the key. Whether you potluck, stop along the roadside to eat, or dine out in a restaurant, follow the suggestions to relax, eat slowly and let a friendly spirit prevail. Enjoy the people around you as well as the food you eat.

Chapter 7

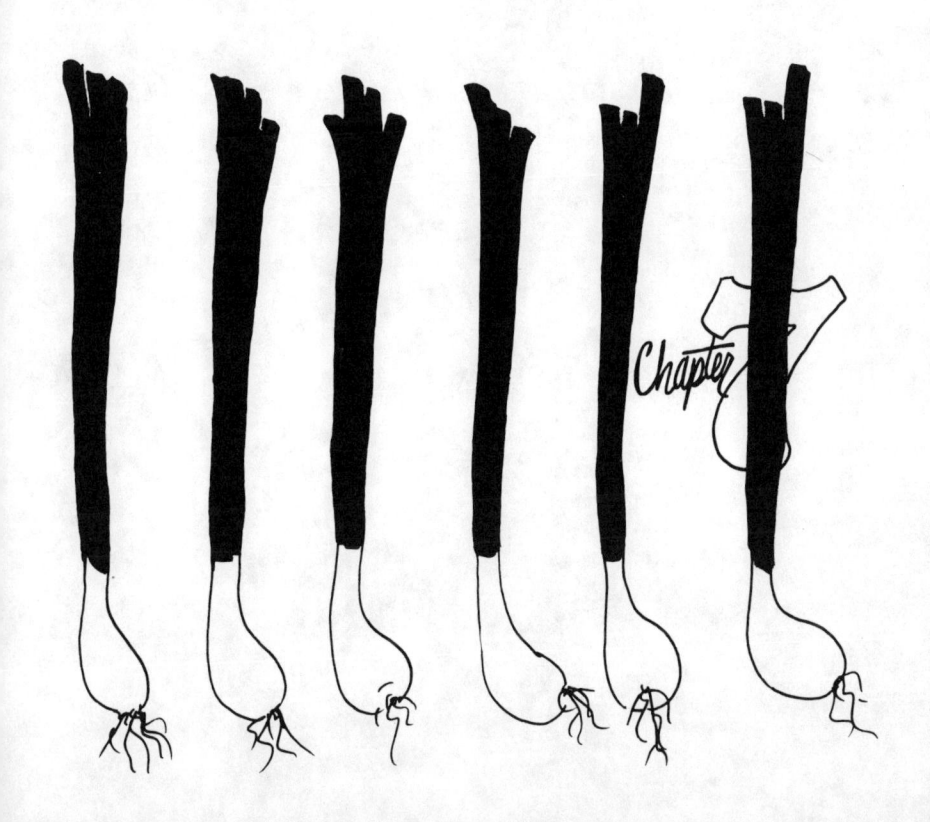

7 MIXING AND MATCHING FOODS

Besides a serene atmosphere for eating meals, as mentioned in the previous chapter, there are ways to combine foods at one meal for improved digestion. A growing number of health practitioners and doctors are publicizing their findings that the body's digestive mechanism may be thwarted by the improper combination of foods which is so common to all types of diets, whether health, natural, or junk oriented.

The reason for this can become very technical, and a number of books are listed in the bibliography which will aid in your understanding should you desire to commit yourself to optional food combining habits. Most vegetarians do not eat with any food combining principles in mind (except for foods in combination that will provide complete protein), and it would be surprising if you adopted this pattern, especially in the early stages of becoming a vegetarian.

Yet a nod has to be made to the principles underlying the practice. Research has determined much about the digestive and assimilative mechanisms at work in the human body, and practitioners of eating, like us, ought to recognize some of the facts. Perhaps it is the manner in which you are mixing your so-called health foods that is preventing you from reaching such eating goals as no disease, proper digestion, increased awareness, less body fat, etc. As with the concept of "the vegan", the food combining plan is a manner of eating worth knowing about and something you may want to try later on.

First, though, here's a quick refresher on what happens during the digestion process. Even before the food gets into the mouth, digestion may begin. There are certain enzymes that are stimulated into action by the very sight and smell of particular foods. Doesn't your mouth "water" at the mere thought of some favorite dish? Within this "water" or saliva, is an enzyme called ptyalin, which begins the breakdown of starches while they are masticated. Then, as the food goes through the digestive cycle (down the esophogus, into the stomach, the small intestine, and eventually is assimilated into or passed out of the body) many different enzymes are employed. Each enzyme performs a different function based on the class of food that is being passed on. For example, pepsin in the stomach acts on proteins and gastric lipase acts on pre-emulsified fats. An Enzyme-Action Table in *Dr. Donsbach's Nutritional Approach to Superhealth* (International Institute of Natural Health Sciences, Inc., Huntington Beach, California. 1980) clearly illustrates the types and functions of enzymes in the human body.

It is the contention of Donsbach and other experts that the indiscriminate use of foods from different categories confuses the body's autonomic mechanisms to such an extent as to render digestion useless. In common terms, bloating, belching, constipation, diarrhea, flatulence, and heartburn are most likely caused by combining foods that are not similar enough in their molecular structures to be digested at the same time.

Dr. Herbert Shelton, perhaps the leading advocate of proper food combining, has classified foods as to the enzyme action necessary for their most efficient use by the body. He has separated foods into these categories:

Proteins: flesh foods, dairy products, nuts, seeds, etc.

Starches: cereals, dry beans, squash, etc.

Green Vegetables: bell pepper, broccoli, okra, etc.

Sweet Fruits: bananas, figs, berries, etc.

Acid Fruits: pineapple, oranges, grapefruit, etc.

Sub-Acid Fruits: apples, pears, grapes, etc.

Fats: cooking oils, butter, cream, lard, etc.

Melons: watermelon, cantaloupe, crenshaw melon, etc.

In his book, *Food Combining Made Easy,* Dr. Shelton describes the action of particular enzymes on particular food groups as physiological catalysts. Each enzyme can produce only one type of digestive action; each can work on only one type of food. The process is so finely tuned that it takes one enzyme to help digest the complex sugar, maltose, and a different one to help digest another sugar, lactose.

Each specific enzyme must have a chance to work on its target food group relatively free from molestation, according to Shelton's theory. This molesting can take the form of emotional upset, too much liquid intake while eating, or more likely the presence of food from a category outside the target group. When this "outside" food makes its arrival, the action of the enzyme can be highly limited or cease altogether. Inadequate digestion of the first food (and probably the second) can be the result.

To avoid this improper digestion, and for the best use per bite of the food we consume, Dr. Shelton recommends some principles of optional eating and good food combining:

1. Eat acids and starches at separate meals
2. Eat protein foods and carbohydrates at different times
3. Eat concentrated protein food alone
4. Proteins and acids should not be consumed at the same time
5. Protein and fats are not a good combination
6. Eat sugars and proteins at different meals
7. Milk should be taken by itself

A food combining chart based on Shelton's principles and those of Dr. William L. Esser is available now at many health food and natural food markets. It simply and attractively delineates the tenets of proper combinations and appears to be a practical aid for the concerned eater. If you cannot find one, try writing to Shangri-La Natural Health Institute of Bonita Springs, Florida 33923 for information. You'll find the following recommendations/advice included on the chart:

— mono meals (a single item of food) will digest more readily than if that article is taken with another kind of food

— water dilutes digestive juices, so should be taken no sooner than fifteen minutes before any meal, thirty minutes after eating fruit, two hours after starch, and four hours after a protein meal

— "desert the desserts"

— if more than one food is eaten at a sitting, these combinations are good: proteins and green vegetables or starches and green vegetables; fair combinations are sweet fruits and sub-acid fruits; sub-acid fruits and acid fruits; and poor combinations are sweet fruits and acid fruits; fruits and green vegetables; starches and acid fruits; protein and starches

— avocado can be eaten with most foods except proteins and melons

— tomatoes can be eaten with green vegetables and proteins

— melons should be eaten alone

These rules may be too limiting for you at this time, but there are folks out there who are trying their best to approach this ideal eating pattern in order to make the most of the food they ingest. Cathy, the owner of a natural food market, who was introduced in Chapter 3, has made the attempt for some time now. She recommends three meals per day for beginners, with one meal fruit only, one meal protein and vegetables, and the third meal starch and vegetables. For anyone who eats only two meals daily, fruit snacks about three hours before or after the meals are good.

Cathy does not always stick to this routine, but she says "I feel much better when I do." She offers these sample menus based on food-combining principles:

1. Steamed vegetables (carrots, broccoli, onions, etc.)
   Brown Rice
2. Tossed Salad
   Whole Wheat Rolls

3. Acorn Squash Stuffed with Millet
   Green Salad
4. Fruit Salad (apples, pears, peaches, raisins and bananas)
5. Stir-Fried Vegetables and Tofu Cubes
6. Tostadas (corn tortilla topped with vegetables, sprouts and guacamole)
7. Vegetable Soup
   Whole Wheat Crackers
8. Curried Vegetables
   Wheat Berries
9. Tofu-Vegetable Casserole
   Green Salad
10. Whole Wheat Pasta
    Vegetable Topping (no tomatoes)

For most of us, this type of eating plan is like "One Step Beyond." Can health really be all *that* important? You have to decide for yourself. Just get as many facts and opinions as you can. Then choose the mode that suits you.

8

before

after

DIETING THE VEGETARIAN WAY

Remember our friend, Ernest? One of the benefits of his changeover from junk food and meat to a basic natural food vegetarian diet was a steady loss of weight. In a month's time, he went from 160 pounds to 145 pounds, which seems to be his normal weight. He fluctuates very little from this plateau as long as he avoids sugar and other highly refined carbohydrates. Whole grains and other unrefined carbohydrates seem to be metabolized at an acceptable rate for his body and those foods make up the bulk of his diet.

Ernest is probably the exception to the rule, though. Many other people appear to put on pounds (or remain the same weight) once they switch over to a meatless diet. Why? The answer, of course, lies within each individual's experience. Some people can eat massive quantities of the richest food and never gain a pound. This is incredibly frustrating to others who seem to add an inch to their hips just by walking by a pastry shop and catching a good whiff of the sugary treats inside. Heredity, activity, conditioning, timing, hormonal secretions, and other physical as well as emotional and mental factors all play a role in weight gain or loss.

Our society places a great deal of emphasis on beauty and glamour. Thin is in and fat is equal to leprosy. Media hype and advertising have conditioned all of us to use the yardstick of svelte pubescent models against our own maturing frames. This pressure is felt the most strongly by women, and they have become ripe for any scheme that will help them approach the ideal established by the likes of Bo Derek, Suzanne Somers, Brook Shields, and the other "10's" on the screen.

Look at the popularity of predigested protein, over-the-counter appetite suppressants, amphetamines, and any of the hundreds of diets and schemes that lead to a yo-yoing of off again-on again inches and pounds. Obviously, the need is for a calm and cool appraisal of our own individual body types within the context of a particular life style, environment, and personal needs.

Obesity is not desirable. It leads to a plethora of health problems and actually shortens the total life span. Excess weight on anyone's frame ought to be eliminated and most experts agree that the only way to maintain an optimal body mass is to actually change dietary habits that lead to or cause the problem in the first place.

Fad diets do work — for a time. Weight is lost when one starts taking in less calories than the body needs to maintain its various life functions. This is fundamental. However, if behavior change is not a part of the program, it is very likely that the conscientious dieter, who sacrificed so much for that three week period of grapefruit and celery, will find the pounds increasing again as soon as the normal eating routine is reestablished.

It is very important to realize what conditions cause us to become or remain overweight. When those conditions are altered, we will have a good chance of finding that utopia so many of us are looking for: eating without the fear (and concomitant tension) that we will look like blimps in the morning.

Kurt W. Donsbach, Ph.D., D.Sc., N.D. D.C., has written many pamphlets, programs, and books on healthful living through correct eating practices. In his latest book (mentioned earlier) *Nutritional Approach to Superhealth,* he outlines the reasons for excess weight gain and provides a proven method for losing pounds. He cites the overuse of refined carbohydrates, which the body readily converts to stored fat, as a prime factor for this country's obesity problem.

Dr. Donsbach also blames an unnatural craving for food caused by an inadequate supply of the basic nutrients, including vitamins, minerals, and proteins. The body will attempt to compensate for the inadequacies by sending hunger signals to the brain. And if the brain is full of fast food slogans and visions of candy bars, the action it takes to satiate that hunger is pretty predictable: More refined carbohydrates and more useless calories.

The Donsbach program revolves around fasting, exercise, a positive mental attitude, food supplements, and a basic diet of natural foods. He recommends a fast to get things started because of the cleansing effect. Other results include breaking old habit patterns, mental clarity, and shrinking the stomach.

The fast, which Donsbach terms liver-kidney-bowel cleansing, is a ten-day program of specific juice, supplement, and food intake requirements designed to take off the first five to ten pounds. After fasting, the "dieter" is directed to a program of nutritionally sound eating that avoids heavy carbohydrate consumption. Dr. Donsbach also believes we should all eat like kings in the morning, princes at noon, and paupers after dark. This allows food to be utilized best at the times the body will actually be needing it. This procedure in itself will help to use up calories instead of adding them in stored fat while we are sleeping overnight.

The Donsbach diet along with a supplement formula he recommends, a positive goal-oriented attitude, and the use of exercise before meals as an appetite depressant can lead the individual to lose weight. But the greater good comes when a person can sustain the important new patterns of eating, which should have been established during the weight-loss period.

Simply avoiding meat is not generally an adequate measure to assure weight loss. As the new vegetarian attempts to learn how to fill up an apparent "hole" in the diet created by the absence of flesh, he/she will quite often devour far too many carbohydrate-laden foods such as rice, beans, potatoes, corn and milk products which can easily be converted to extra weight. Meat, although it contains a very high ratio of fat to protein availability, is not as apt to add pounds to the frame. Fat absorption takes up to fifteen times longer to happen than carbohydrate utilization, thus fat can be used much more efficiently without adding to the body mass. It also creates a "full" feeling in the stomach for a longer period of time.

Statistically, though, vegetarians as a rule are much less prone to plumpness than those whose diets consist of meat and convenience foods. The simple fact to remember is that when you consume more calories than your body needs for the energy it expends, you will gain weight in the form of stored fat. Whether the calories come from Wonder Bread or Wah-Guru-Chew Naturally Sweet Candy, the body has to compensate for the intake with adequate energy output. In short, health food or junk food — work it off or get fat!

One internationally known nutritionist, Paavo Airola, Ph.D., N.D. recommends a *low* protein diet to help lose weight. In his book *How to Get Well*, he outlines a program for optimal health based on a diet that includes seeds, nuts, grains, vegetables and fruits, 75% of which should be eaten raw. He does not recommend eating meat for good health.

Dr. Airola also suggests fasting for weight loss. He calls for a *repeated* seven to ten day fast. Between the fasting periods, he recommends a great deal of physical exercise, hot and cold shower treatments, apple cider vinegar with each meal, a low protein diet, avoiding all sugar, white flour, salt, coffee, tea, and alcohol. Along with this, he has devised an effective vitamin/mineral supplement formula, taken after meals to minimize the appetite stimulant effect of certain B vitamins and to achieve what he feels is a correct balance of these substances in the body. According to Airola, a body not starved for nutrients will not "need" food as much.

In addition, he advises eating several small meals during the day rather than the three large "squares" that are customary. Plenty of the following foods should be included: brewer's yeast, kelp, and cold-pressed vegetable oils.

Such a program sounds severe to anyone who is used to the merry-go-round cycle of junk food, diet, junk food, diet... But Airola has treated many ills by nutritional methods and claims results. Naturally, he recommends seeing your own doctor before starting any radical new routine in eating. However, he cautions that you go to a physician who spouts a little more than the typical high protein-low carbohydrate/fat lines. He feels that this can cause undue harm to the system.

If you lose weight, this is often the point at which you confront your eating habits and begin to see a connection between what goes into your body and what you become. Many nutritional doctors believe that bad eating habits not only equal obesity but they also lead to such serious health problems as cancer, heart disease, mental illness, hypoglycemia, colitis, etc.

Each nutritionist recommends his or her own program, but almost all advise natural food consumption with low animal protein. There may be a time in the future when a great many more of us will seek the advice of these holistic practitioners who can provide personalized diet/exercise plans as a means to ameliorate or prevent any number of health problems, not simply overweight bodies.

juices

Chapter 9

9 FASTING

Imagine going without food for a five, ten, even up to a thirty day period. Surely death would come knocking at your door. Most people feel this way about fasting, if they have never heard of the concept. Our friend, Ernest, felt strongly that he could never survive a fast of over a day's duration. Even when he followed an exemplary chemical-free vegetarian diet, he still believed he had to have a certain amount of solid food each day.

"Where would I get my energy?" he asked. "I work hard at my job, you know. Fasting sounds good for some people, but I don't think I could handle it."

His conclusion was correct. With a negative approach he couldn't handle it. A positive attitude and a supportive environment are two key factors in completing a successful fast.

Ernest found this out just recently. Although his life situation hadn't changed much from the time when he "knew" he'd die if he tried to go without food, nevertheless he was able to accomplish a ten-day fast, working a physically demanding job with little or no stress to his bodily functions.

Yet, why make such a sacrifice? What's the point anyway? What can one get out of fasting besides hunger pangs?

Plenty.

Maybe you have no intention to fast, but any book that attempts to show the options available to those who would move away from the life-depleting end of the eating continuum should at least touch on this concept. After all, many health practitioners, whether they be vegetarian or not, have recommended a dietary regimen that includes fasting one day out of each week just to give the body a rest. Raw vegetable and/or fruit juice fasting has many proponents.

Of course there is no intent here on the part of the authors to take the place of medical doctors or other health specialists who may now be advising you. Consult your physician before beginning any fast. You might also want to review some of the resources listed in this chapter.

How to Keep Healthy and Happy by Fasting is one of those books. It was written by Salem Kirban, a health practitioner who discovered the benefits of fasting after he was forty years old. Today, he and his wife regularly fast, usually one day per week but occasionally for longer periods also. He claims there are seventeen good reasons to fast:

1. To lower blood pressure
2. To lower cholesterol level
3. To clean out the body
4. To give the digestive system a rest
5. To give the body time to heal itself
6. To relieve nervousness and tension
7. To sleep better
8. To regulate bowel movements and provide better elimination

9. To make one more alert
10. To sharpen the mental processes
11. To slow the aging process
12. To save money
13. To feel and look better physically
14. To lose weight quickly and easily
15. To improve marital life
16. To help eliminate smoking and drinking
17. To learn the will of God

Amazing isn't it? By not eating, by going against Mama's admonition to "Clean your plate" you can actually be a better person — physically, mentally, and spiritually.

Some medical doctors are now beginning to prescribe short fasts for their patients. It is the wise M.D. who understands that the body heals itself and whatever aids in that process should be part of the total treatment.

Otto Buchinger, M.D., author of *Everything You Want to Know about Fasting,* has supervised over 70,000 fasts, and recommends the practice for patients who are overweight, have rheumatism, heart disease, suffer from stress and nervous debility, skin disorders, diseases of the digestive or respiratory organs, kidney and bladder diseases, disorders common to females, allergies, and certain eye diseases such as iritis or retinitis.

"Fasting is. . .a royal road to healing for anyone who agrees to take it for the recovery and regeneration of the body, mind and spirit," Dr. Buchinger writes.

Whether you take the road is up to you and your own medical advisor. There is evidence to indicate that the elimination of solid food and its replacement with specific fruit or vegetable juices can and does lead to overall improvement for many individuals.

When Ernest found he was ready to try fasting, he had no specific complaints about his life other than a little extra weight. He happened to read a friend's copy of William F. Burroughs' pamphlet on *The Master Cleanser* and the idea caught fire. A fast, he felt, would help him achieve more discipline in his life and he could once again assume responsibility for what he consumed.

Ernest talked about the Burroughs' fast with several friends and three of them decided to try it at the same time. None of them had fasted anywhere near the ten-day duration this called for, but they felt if they supported one another they could do it.

"It was amazing," he said after the period was over. "I wasn't at all hungry after the second day. I continued my gardening job with no cut-backs and I continued eliminating waste from my body for the entire ten days. Believe it or not, I had more energy than when I eat normally. The three of us who fasted together didn't really want to stop. I was more surprised by my behavior than I've been about anything else I've ever done. I felt good about myself and my body and I lost fifteen pounds that I didn't need to carry around. My partners lost weight steadily, too. We all plan to fast this way again in the future – when the time is right."

The "right" time is definitely an important point for anyone thinking about a fast, especially one that lasts for ten days. Having "fasting partners" is an excellent method to keep you at it. Any number of support groups have proven the benefits of having others in your corner when attempting to change deep-seated behavior patterns. It is also helpful to have a goal (lose ten pounds, go for five days, relieve stomach pains, etc.). But take each day at a time so that maintaining the fast does not become a stressful event.

One of the main ideas behind fasting is to eliminate tensions. Avoid people who are negative in their approach to life, especially if they are going to be doomsaying your efforts. Many a faster has gone for the cookie jar because he or she has picked up the negative vibrations of a loved one who does not understand the possibilities for good that not eating brings. The longer and more often you fast, the stronger your resolve will become.

However, will power is not necessarily a factor after the first or second day of juice fasting. Miraculously, it seems, you are not hungry. If you feel the need for an energy boost, you start to equate this with drinking more of your juice and not with a call to candy bars or other foods.

A great number of published materials are available on the benefits of this or that fast. Reading just a small portion of the books, pamphlets and articles can be confusing. You might ask: Should I drink only water? Should I try a vegetable juice fast or are fruit juices better? By educating yourself on the options and seeking valid practical and medical advice, you will probably be able to find a fasting technique to your liking. It took several attempts before Ernest found the Burroughs' fast which calls for a special lemon drink (ingredients are listed later on in this chapter).

Any fast you choose should fit the needs of your life style, but there are a few general principles to guide you in your quest for your personal fasting routine. These "rules" have been compiled from the works of several health writers and many folks who have gone through the fasting experience.

For one thing, you should eat lightly for perhaps two or three days prior to the fast. This helps bring about the change in attitude you'll need to be successful, setting your body and mind for doing with less. Eat your normal diet — just lighten the load.

Don't attempt a water only fast unless your doctor agrees you can handle it and your body has been cleaned out. Living on just water is a harsh experience even for the most accomplished faster. Drinking water with juices is beneficial, however. Fruit juices should be diluted with distilled water by at least fifty percent. Straight fruit juice is too concentrated in sugar.

Fasts of 30 to 45 days have been accomplished by many people, but such long-term fasts throw off the body's digestive and elimination systems and should not be attempted without expert supervision.

The primary benefit of fasting is the cleansing of the intestinal tract. This is the area of the body where solid waste is deposited for eventual elimination through peristaltic action. Quite often the lack of solid food intake cuts the body's normal signalling for this action to take place. Since the cleansing of the intestine is what we want to accomplish, it is usually necessary to use some supplemental means to keep eliminating the waste. Some experts say to use enemas, others tell you to rely on herbal laxatives which stimulate the body to act more normally. Keeping bowel movements going every day is of paramount importance.

In order to be of any benefit, other than a good rest for the body's digestive organs, a fast should last at least a week. For the first attempt, however, three days is probably best.

People with chronic health problems like hypoglycemia or diabetes should take care when fasting as great fluctuations in blood sugar might result. It is especially necessary for these people to consult their doctors before trying any major changes in their eating habits. Fasting is supposed to heal, not destroy. So take care.

Breaking the fast properly is as important as the actual fast. Many of the cleansing benefits can be lost if one jumps back into regular food after going without for so long. The body isn't ready to digest heavy proteins, carbohydrates, and fats after its rest and that food could end up clogging the intestines with undigested masses. There should be a gradual transition – into the fasting period and out of it once again.

In *Fasting as a Way of Life* by Allan Cott, M.D. you'll find a number of "after-the-fast menus" that may be helpful. The paperback book also includes an extensive bibliography, if you want to do further research on the subject of fasting.

As you try your own fast, you will no doubt find techniques that will help you make it successful. Listen to your mind, body, and spirit and know that many others have used fasting as a means for improving their lives in all of those areas.

Just what do people consume when fasting? The Burroughs' fast consists of a lemon drink designed to clean the system, take off pounds, and rebuild the body while maintaining a good energy level and causing few fluctuations in blood sugar. Burroughs suggests drinking as much of the "lemonade" as often as you want for ten days. To prepare the drink use the juice of 1 lemon, adding it to ten ounces of distilled water. Stir in two tablespoons of grade C maple syrup and a dash of cayenne pepper.

Many people have had successful experiences with this particular fast. It is especially effective for weight loss. And more often than not, the participants want to go on longer than the ten days – they feel so healthy, energetic, and clear in the head. As Ernest put it: "The stuff tastes good, too. What a bonus!"

Cathy, the natural food merchant, has tried many different types of fasts, and she recommends the following seven-day regimen:

Day One: Use comfrey tea to clean out the stomach.

Day Two: Drink diluted pineapple juice to cleanse the small intestine.

Day Three: Drink beet juice to cleanse the liver.

Day Four: Drink carrot juice as a general cleanser.

Day Five: Drink green juice (which is a combination of juices from any of the green vegetables such as spinach, parsley, cucumber, bell peppers, etc.) to begin to build up the system after cleansing.

Day Six: Back to comfrey tea which can also supplement any of the juices throughout the fast.

Day Seven: For this final day, drink distilled water and relax.

Cathy found this to be a very positive fast for her and explained that her doctor's support helped a great deal in making the experience beneficial.

Fasts are recommended by other health devotees to ameliorate specific physical problems. The authors make no claims as to their effectiveness, but for your information some of them are given here:

Watermelon fasting is said to be good for kidney and bladder ailments, probably because of that fruit's diuretic effects.

Grape juice diluted 50% with water is said to be a tremendous cleanser when used during a short fast.

All fruit and vegetable juices have beneficial effects on the human system, according to Dr. Norman W. Walker who wrote the book *Fresh Vegetable and Fruit Juices*. While not calling for a juice fast, Walker does give the reader many juice formulas that could be used in anyone's routine for improved health.

Whether or not you use juices in a non-food fasting situation depends on you. Like a change of diet or life style, it is something to at least consider. But don't rush it. If you are a vegetarian novice or new to the concepts of natural health care, the ideas on eating can be confusing enough. Absorb the information at your own pace.

Remember also that this chapter is intended to provide only introductory material on fasting and what some individuals and practitioners suggest. Consult your doctor before you attempt any of the programs described herein.

→ First we start with 3 eggs, 2 spoons, and 1½ scoops of sunflower seeds; stir vigorously — gesticulation counts in preparation!

10.

10 BACK TO THE KITCHEN

By this time, maybe you've freaked out and cleaned your cupboards and refrigerator of all additive-tainted foods and meat products. So now what are you going to do? What will you prepare for your meals?

Don't make lima bean loaf! That was Ernest's first try at vegetarian cookery and it almost sent him right back to frozen TV dinners. As he described the dish "It was a disgusting green mass of dry vegetation. I sure couldn't make a sandwich out of the stuff. My dog wouldn't even touch it."

Today Ernest is a good vegetarian and natural food cook. But that's eight years after the first attempts. Luckily for you there are now a number of excellent vegetarian/natural food cookbooks on the market. Many include good sections on proteins and proper combining of food for complete proteins, whole grain and dried legume preparation, suggestions for daily menus, glossaries, and healthier substitutes for refined foods like sugar and white flour.

Ernest found *Laurel's Kitchen* (Bantam) and *The Deaf Smith Country Cookbook* (Collier Books) to be of the most help when he began. Later he used *Tassajara Cooking* (Random House/Shabhala) which does not list precise measurements or ingredients so the cook is free to use his own experience and taste in creating vegetarian dishes. Experiment with a few of the cookbooks and you'll soon have a favorite.

This chapter includes some recipes and meal ideas that will help you get started. They have been chosen for their practicality and taste and are proven. If you bring fresh, natural ingredients to the kitchen, these dishes should provide you with some fine eating.

First, though, you'll need to have explanations for some of the food terms that you'll be seeing here and in other publications or places (stores, restaurants, etc.) where natural foods/vegetarian meals are described. Try not to judge the foods before you've tried them in several recipes. Many taste much different from what you may be used to, but they'll grow on you.

FOOD TERMS

Agar - Agar — A gelatin product made from seaweed which can be used in place of commercial gelatin; available in flakes, powder or stick (bar) form.

Arrowroot Powder — Use this thickening agent in place of cornstarch. Made from the root of the arrowroot plant, it's a good source of protein.

Brewer's Yeast — This nutritional yeast is not for baking. It's a great source of some B vitamins and protein, and can be added to a variety of foods. Some brands have a strong taste, however, so experiment to find one you prefer.

Brown Rice — A whole grain rice that has not been stripped of its bran and much of its nutritional value as is the case with white rice.

Bulghur Wheat — A whole grain that is parboiled, dried, then cracked. When soaked it becomes fluffy and can be used in many dishes.

Carob — A very popular substitute for chocolate which comes from the seed pods of the carob tree and is naturally sweet. It's often sold in powder and chip forms.

Certified Raw Milk — Not readily available in all states, this unpasteurized milk must meet government standards for purity. Animals must be tested for disease, particularly tuberculosis, and dairies must meet health and cleanliness standards before raw milk (and raw milk products) can be labeled "certified."

Cheese (Natural) — Made without artificial color and preservatives.

Date Sugar — Usually available in "health food stores" or natural food markets, this white sugar substitute is made from dried, ground dates.

Kefir — A milk product which can be described as "liquid yogurt."

Kelp — Sea vegetables processed into a powder which supplies essential iodine and many other minerals. It's a complete protein (containing all essential amino acids).In powder or granulated form, this is a good substitute for salt.

Milk Powder (non-instant) — A highly concentrated product that provides additional nutrients in many recipes. Non-instant milk powder is naturally sweet and in various baked goods reduces the amount of other types of sweetners needed.

Millet — A grain that can be used in place of rice, providing low-gluten protein.

Miso — A fermented soybean-based paste which is easily digested. It makes an excellent base for soup broth and is a good source of protein. However, it's very salty and a little goes a long way.

Pita (Bible bread or Greek flat bread) — A quick-baked bread, circular in shape, with an air pocket in the middle. The bread can be cut in two and the pouch stuffed with various sandwich fillings.

Sprouts — The first growth of seeds and beans. These are among the freshest foods you can consume and they are high in nutritional value. Note the suggestions for various types of sprouts in Chapter 5. A word of caution: Don't use tomato seeds, eggplant or potato sprouts. They're poisonous.

Tamari — A soy sauce, naturally fermented by aging for two years in wooden kegs. It's often used in place of salt for seasoning.

Tempeh — A meat substitute made from soybeans which are soaked, cooked, and innoculated with a mold (tempeh culture). The filaments of edible mold connect the soybeans into a meaty textured food.

Tofu — A soybean curd made from soybean milk which is curdled in much the same way as cow's milk is curdled for cottage cheese. This is a bland food with a light texture which can be used in place of cheese or even eggs. Eight ounces of tofu is equal in protein to seven ounces of hamburger at a fraction of the cost. (There are a variety of Tofu Cookbooks on the market.)

Unrefined, Cold-Pressed Oils — Unsaturated vegetable oils are extracted without heat, bleaching, deodorizing or use of chemical solvents, all of which destroy nutrients. You'll find unrefined corn, safflower, olive, sesame, peanut, soy and sunflower oils in natural food stores and sometimes on supermarket shelves.

Yogurt — A milk product made by using a "starter" that allows special bacteria to grow in a host medium. You can prepare your own yogurt, using directions supplied with a commercial yogurt maker or you can follow instructions in various cookbooks. If you buy commercially prepared yogurt, be sure to check the label so that you get plain yogurt without sugar or other sweetners.

Ready to try your hand at cooking? Here are a few easy recipes that can provide a whole or part of a meal.

CHEESE-BAKED VEGETABLES

Steam any combination of vegetables that are in season. Place the steamed vegetables in a baking dish. Mix together ½ cup melted butter with ¼ cup tamari and pour over vegetables. Sprinkle with grated cheese and bake at 350 degrees until cheese melts. Serve over brown rice.

CURRIED VEGETABLES

Quickly stir-fry in sesame oil chopped onion, broccoli, carrot, zuccini, bell pepper (in proportions suitable for the number of people to be served). Season with garlic powder, cayenne pepper, curry powder and a little honey or maple syrup. Sprinkle seasonings carefully at first and test for your own taste.

FRUIT SALAD

Combine any seasonal fresh fruits with cashews, almonds, walnuts, and/or pecans. Add raisins or dates and sprinkle with raw coconut. Mix with a dressing made of 1 cup of plain yogurt, about ¼ cup honey or maple syrup, cinnamon and nutmeg to taste.

NUTBURGERS

Combine 1 cup ground cashews, 1 cup ground walnuts, 1 cup cooked brown rice, ½ cup wheat germ, 2 teaspoons of curry powder, 1 teaspoon of garlic powder, a dash of cayenne pepper. Form patties of the mixture and place them on an oiled cookie sheet. Bake at 350 degrees for 35 minutes.

PITA PIZZAS

Slice one pita horizontally and toast the two circles lightly. Layer each half with enough tomato sauce to cover, sliced mushrooms, finely chopped onion, green pepper and other vegetables of your choice. Season to taste and top with grated cheese. Bake in moderate over for a few minutes until cheese melts.

SOY BURGERS

Grind cooked soybeans to a pulp in a blender, forming enough pulp for the number of people to be served (you might compare with a similar mass of ground meat). Add enough wheat germ to stiffen. Mix in chopped onions and bell peppers to taste, adding any seasonings you prefer. Fry in sesame oil until brown on both sides.

STUFFED ACORN SQUASH

Cut a squash in half and scoop out the seeds. Prepare a stuffing by combining 1 cup millet and 3 cups of water in a pan. Bring to a boil, cover and simmer for ½ hour. Then mix in finely chopped carrots, onion, garlic and zucchini. Season to taste with basil, oregano, thyme, and tamari. Stuff the squash and bake at 350 degrees for 45 minutes.

TABOULI

Soak two cups of bulghur wheat in one cup of warm water for an hour. Then add the following to the fluffy grain and toss together: ½ cup chopped scallions; 1 cup chopped parsley; 2 medium tomatoes, chopped; ¼ cup lemon juice; ½ cup unrefined oil; 1 teaspoon garlic salt; and sea salt and pepper to taste. Refrigerate and serve as a salad or complete meal. Garbanzo beans can be added as a protein complement for the wheat.

TOFU CASSEROLE

Mash and stir together a pound of tofu with seasonings of your choice (cayenne pepper, garlic powder, onion powder, basil, tamari, or some other you prefer). Spread half of the tofu mixture on the bottom of a baking dish. Then layer an assortment of steamed or sauteed vegetables over the tofu. Spread the other half of the tofu on top. Bake 20 minutes at 350 degrees.

VEGETABLE QUICHE

Precook vegetables in season such as asparagus, beans broccoli, or cauliflower until just tender. Place the cooked vegetables in the bottom of a buttered pie plate or in a baked pie shell. Then beat together three or four eggs, ¾ cup of milk, 6-8 ounces of grated cheese, and minced onions and seasonings to taste. Pour the mixture over the vegetables and bake at 350 degrees for 30 minutes or until set.

VEGETABLE SOUP

Combine two quarts of water with one vegetable bouillon cube and four cups of chopped fresh vegetables of your choice. Cook until the vegetables are soft and season to taste. (Note: You can use leftover cooked vegetables and broth from vegetables in a soup. Add a little water and seasonings to taste. Cook until the flavors blend. You can also add brown rice, noodles or soy grits to the soup.)

Once in awhile you'll want snacks, beverages, and desserts and you'll find a variety of these in the natural food/vegetarian cookbooks now available. To have something on hand, though try these:

SNACKS and BEVERAGES

CHEESE CUBES

Prepare small cubes of different types of natural cheeses and keep them in a plastic bag in the refrigerator. Then if you are tempted to go for a candy bar or cookies you can get a quick bite of protein instead.

FRESH VEGETABLE SNACKS

Cut up any types of fresh vegetables you prefer and store them in plastic containers in the refrigerator for between meal munching.

TOASTED TAMARI NUTS/SEEDS

Use equal amounts of raw peanuts, cashews, almonds, and sunflower seeds and soak them in tamari for about 30 minutes. Then drain the excess tamari from the mixture and place the nuts and seeds on an ungreased cookie sheet. Bake for about 40 minutes in a 325 degree oven.

TRAIL MIX

Mix together ½ cup *each* of raw sunflower seeds, peanuts, almonds, raisins, and carob chips (if you like them). Store in a tightly-closed container. You can experiment with other types of nuts and seeds, too, combining them for snacks.

FRUIT COOLER

This kind of beverage is best prepared in a blender. Combine a cup (rounded) of fresh fruit, ½ cup of fruit juice, and ½ cup of crushed ice. Blend all the ingredients. You can add honey, maple syrup or vanilla for flavoring if you like.

SHAKES

Start with a cup of honey ice cream and ½ cup of milk for each shake. Blend with fresh fruits (banana, peach, or strawberries, for example) or use carob powder. Peanut butter is good, too. Whip until you have a smooth, creamy shake.

CANDIES and DESSERTS

CAROB FUDGE

Don't cook this mixture. Simply combine 1 cup carob powder with ½ cup of honey, ½ cup of coconut oil, and ½ teaspoon of almond extract or vanilla. Blend until creamy. Then add ½ cup of seeds or nuts if desired. Press the mixture into a buttered pan and chill until firm. Cut in small pieces.

PEANUT-CAROB CANDY

It's best to use your hands for this mixture. Combine 1 cup each of peanut butter, honey, dry milk powder and peanuts. Press the stiff mixture into a buttered pan. Then combine ½ pound of melted carob chips with a teaspoon of melted butter. Pour the "sauce" over the peanut mixture and refrigerate until firm enough to cut in squares.

FRUIT CREPES

You can fill crepes (use your favorite recipe to make up a batch, substituting some whole wheat pastry flour for white flour) with a variety of fruits for an excellent dessert. Mash strawberries or peaches with a dash of salt for a filling. Combine berries with yogurt (1 cup of each for four fillings), adding cinnamon, nutmeg, or other spice of your choice. You can combine chunky applesauce with raisins and nuts, plus your favorite spice and fill dessert crepes.

PEANUT-OAT COOKIES

Cream together:
- ½ cup butter
- 1 cup honey

Add:
- 1 beaten egg

Mix in:
- ½ cup peanut butter
- 1½ cups whole wheat flour
- 1 cup rolled oats
- ½ teaspoon salt
- 1 cup peanuts

Drop the mixture by teaspoonfuls on a lightly greased cookie sheet and bake for 15-20 minutes in moderate oven.

RAISIN-CUSTARD

Add 1 cup of raisins to 3 cups of whole milk and store in the refrigerator overnight. The next day, blend the mixture and add it to 4 large or 5 medium eggs, beaten. Add 1 teaspoon vanilla and ¼ teaspoon salt. Pour into custard cups and sprinkle with nutmeg. Place the cups in a baking pan with about an inch of hot water. Bake at 300-325 degrees for about an hour or until set (to test insert a knife in the center; when knife comes out clean the custard has set).

Salad

11.

11 COPING AS A VEGETARIAN

Here is a scene that might be all too familiar to you one day. Ernest went to the home of an acquaintance for a social gathering and the host came up to him to be hospitable. The conversation went something like this:

HOST: Hi, I see you don't have anything to drink. Can I get you some pop or something?

ERN: Uh, no thank you. I'm not really thirsty, yet. I'll get some water later.

HOST: How about one of those little frankfurters or those bacon-wrapped goodies. I made them myself.

ERN: Well, they look good, but I'm not into meat.

HOST: Oh, uh, well. . .how come? I mean are you on a health kick? I guess you're one of those health food freaks, huh?

ERN: Actually, I am concerned about healthful living, but I don't consider that freakish.

HOST: Yeah, but being so pure – isn't that pretty difficult?

ERN: Oh, I do quite well thank you. My diet is varied – more than adequate.

HOST: *What can you eat?*

ERN: I can eat whatever I choose. Nobody's forcing me to conform to some exclusive club. Vegetarians are just people, you know.

HOST: *I couldn't do it. Eating salads everyday isn't my idea of a good time.*

ERN: Mine either.

HOST: *Honestly, now wouldn't you like a juicy steak sometime? Don't you find all that celery boring?*

ERN: No, but I'm finding you to be.

The American vegetarian exists in a world that is not geared for his/her habits. It is imperative that a method of coping with the greater society be developed if one is not to give way to the pressures of "junksters." A major benefit derived from being a "health food nut" is a sense of well-being and reduced tension, *if* the practitioner can learn to handle confrontations.

Parents, friends, strangers — they'll all have some comments about your freely chosen path. How you deal with non-vegetarians depends on your personality and experience. You can be assertive or aggressive like Ernest or be passive and avoid all possible situations that could cause tension. The important factor is not to allow yourself to become depressed because of your eating habits. Counteract negative influences with positive thoughts/actions. Remember you are doing what's right for you — no one else. You have the right to do right without explaining yourself to anyone.

Perhaps the general answers to the questions below will help you exist in what might appear at times to be a hostile world.

Q. *Will a vegetarian diet supply me with sufficient protein?*
A. A lot of Americans eat far too much protein for their activity level. Experts say that the daily need for the maintenance of cellular growth and repair is anywhere from 35-65 grams of protein per day. This range would change for different body weights, stress levels, physical exertion, etc.

Vegetable proteins are equal to or superior to animal proteins when they are properly combined to supply the nine essential amino acids which the body cannot "manufacture" or synthesize on its own. These must be present to be utilized as the body's building blocks.

Vegetarians must educate themselves as to proper food combining so that all the essential amino acids will be present. Legumes (dried beans) with whole grains, legumes with seeds, and whole grains with milk products are three combinations which will supply complete protein for the human body.

These sources give a fairly in-depth study of the protein question and should clarify the issue for you: *Laurel's Kitchen* (A Handbook for Vegetarian Cookery & Nutrition) by Laurel Robertson, Carol Flinders and Bronwen Godfrey (Nilgiri Press/Bantam, 1976); *Diet for a Small Planet* by Frances Moore Lappe, Revised Edition, (Ballentine Books, 1975); *Protein for Vegetarians* by Gary and Steve Null and staff (Pyramid Books, 1975).

Q. *I know people who have eaten meat, sugar, anything they wanted for 50-60 years. They haven't suffered for it. Why not?*
A. It is impossible to say why one person thrives on a particular diet that would virtually kill another — unless you know each person's make-up, attitude, physical problems, emotional stress, etc. As has been pointed out in previous chapters, an individual has to make his or her own decisions. What's right for one may not be right for the other.

Q. *My spouse doesn't want to give up his Big Mac and fries. I see this as life-depleting food and he doesn't care. How can I get him to change his ways and become more conscious of what he eats?*

A. We all run on different life clocks. The need for change in one person's life will not necessarily be the same need for another. When one partner strikes out on a new path without the other, tremendous pressure will be exerted on the relationship. This is especially true of a change in food consumption habits which are so closely tied to a particular life style.

If one member of a couple truly feels that the habits of the other are working to his/her detriment, it is almost impossible not to say something, criticize, or prod toward a more healthful way of life. Should the prodded individual not be ready for change, sparks could fly and habits could become even more set.

Try an approach that teaches by example. Model the type of behavior you feel is more appropriate. And if you control the kitchen (food buying, preparation, etc.) slip in substitute items slowly and discretely. Don't shove it down someone's throat. Let the other person learn on his or her own. Change is not simple for a person who wants it and it is almost life threatening to someone who doesn't. Be patient if you expect to get results.

Q. *Can children live on a vegetarian diet?*

A. Certainly. Just make certain that the youngster is eating from a wide variety of foods. The conscientious parent will also want to monitor the combinations necessary to achieve a balanced protein intake, as was stated before. Of course, if the child is eating milk products and eggs, the worry about adequate protein (and concern about getting certain vitamins like B_{12}) should be eliminated. Remember that whole societies have lived healthy lives on a natural food, vegetarian regimen.

When it comes to treats and snacks for kids, parents need to use their imaginations to find something exciting for their children to eat. There are many good recipes available now for natural desserts and snacks and children can get involved in a creative cook's kitchen. It's a good opportunity for families to become closer. To paraphrase an old saying: The family that cooks together may stay together.

Q. *What if a person is really strict about a natural food/vegetarian diet? Is it really possible to go out for dinner?*

A. Yes, but more than likely you'll end up at the house of a friend who eats in the same manner. If you are really strict, you'll have problems even in restaurants with salad bars since so many wash their produce in a chemical-based bath designed to take the brown out of lettuce and put the snap back in celery. Over the past decade, however, the number of totally natural food restaurants has expanded greatly. There are even fast natural food spots showing up here and there. As the number of vegetarians increases so do the number of businesses catering to our specific needs.

Q. *Doesn't it take a long time to fix vegetarian meals?*

A. If your meals usually consist of frozen foods that you pop in the microwave or instant foods from a box or can, then of course preparation time will increase when you change to natural foods. But a vegetarian meal doesn't have to take any longer to get on the table than a meat-centered meal once you get used to another way of cooking. Planning, getting the right utensils, and learning about natural foods will help you make efficient use of your time in the kitchen.

Q. *I don't know the first thing about whole grains and dried beans and other natural foods. Where do I get that information?*

A. Unless you come from a rural background, you may be like many urban folks who have never even seen some of the ingredients listed in vegetarian/natural food recipes. But a number of the cookbooks mentioned in earlier chapters and in the bibliography have sections describing various foods. Also, don't be afraid to ask questions when you go into a natural foods market or co-op.

Usually someone can help identify the different grains, beans, flours, nuts, seeds, etc. and briefly explain how they are used.

Q. *Are there any recommended recipes or dishes for the neophyte?*

A. Many people begin the changeover to vegetarianism by substituting milk, cheese and egg dishes for the traditional meat courses. This assures them of protein and the taste is at least familiar.

Q. *Do I need special equipment to get started — I've seen some pretty expensive items in "health food" stores.*

A. You've probably seen food processors which *can* cost a lot. If you can afford one, buy one, but you can get along very well with a good knife and a blender. A well-balanced knife can make a big difference to you, if you've never owned one. You need a knife that will work well for cutting all types of vegetables. Try a restaurant supply house for this and other hardware. You should have a good blender also because you'll use it almost daily for grinding nuts and seeds, making soups, concocting new drinks like smoothies and shakes, creating mayonnaise and other dressings for salad, and even manufacturing your own peanut butter.

Q. *What else will I need in the kitchen?*

A. These will make your food preparation easier and less time-consuming:

— *a pressure cooker.* Dried beans almost demand pressure cooking. The conventional method involves soaking the beans over night in water, then simmering them for up to four hours on the stove. With a pressure cooker, the beans need only to be washed, placed in the pot with three-four times the amount of water, brought to 15 pounds pressure, and cooked for thirty to sixty minutes. Whole grains can also be cooked in the pressure cooker, although they can usually be done quite readily in a good stainless steel pot. Alan Hooker, owner of the well-known gourmet natural food restaurant in Ojai, California, suggests in his book *Vegetarian Gourmet Cookery* that you use a pressure pot for nearly all vegetables. The fast cooking time retains flavor, color, and vital nutrients.

— *a cutting board and a hand grater (or the cranktype).* You'll need the board and grater for vegetables and many recipes call for grated cheeses.

— *a stiff brush.* Be sure to use this to wash the pesticide residue off vegetables and fruits.

— *a strainer or collander.* This utensil has any number of uses when washing or draining foods.

— *a stainless steel vegetable steamer.* This is inexpensive and a good device for quick-cooking vegetables to retain their goodness.

— *a wok.* It will take a little experience to use one correctly, but it, too, helps keep nutrients in food.

— *stainless steel pots and pans, and cast iron skillets.* There is some evidence to indicate that aluminum may be poisoning many of us by cooking in that type of metal. Studies have shown that cooking in copper pots destroys vitamin C present in food. Besides good stainless steel is a joy to use in the kitchen.

— *glass baking pans.* (avoid aluminum.)

— *a commercial yogurt maker or your own homemade system.* You can buy a yogurt maker at a reasonable price and a number of cookbooks tell you how to make yogurt in your own containers.

— *cannisters or glass jars*. You'll need plenty of containers to store natural grains, flour, legumes, dried fruits, nuts, seeds, and possibly herbs.

— *a tea kettle*. What's a kitchen without one that whistles?

— *a juicer*. This can be a very expensive item, but it is a piece of equipment you might want to purchase if you are interested in fasting or juice therapy. There are new brands on the market now that are fairly reasonable, are easy to clean, and get a good juice per pulp ratio. Check around for used juicers as well. Investigate before you buy.

Q. Am I really going to be able to recognize a difference in the taste of natural vegetarian meals compared to convenience foods?

A. Well, after a few weeks of eating properly prepared natural foods, most people do not want meals with ingredients that are overprocessed, full of chemicals that have been added primarily for longer shelf life and cosmetic purposes. However, if your tastebuds demand TV dinners, Oreos, artificially flavored Jell-O, cake mixes, packaged macaroni and cheese, Spaghetti-O's and Pork and Beans from cans, Pepsi, Coke and instant coffee, then by all means get on with eating the "glop and guck" meals as John and Karen Hess describe the mainstream eating habits in *The Taste of America* (Viking).

Q. One final question — of a philosophical nature. Why do some people cite world hunger and food shortages as a reason for eating the natural food/vegetarian way?

A. The United Nations has predicted there will be a shortage of 100 million tons of food for the world's people by the year 2000. Dozens of relief organizations in industrialized nations have called for people to change their eating habits so that they consume less meat.

The rich industrial nations feed as much protein grain to animals as the rest of the world population eats directly. If Americans cut their meat-eating by just ten percent, there would be enough grain available to feed 60 million people. Over two-thirds of our farm land is used to feed livestock while the remaining is used to grow food for human consumption.

Whether advocating vegetarianism or not, a number of religious groups, world-wide service agencies, and health organizations have called for programs of responsible eating, asking that citizens – particularly overfed Americans – cut back on foods and waste, and at the same time eat better with simple diets.

Squash anyone?

12.

1 2 3 4 5 6

12 ERNEST TALK

Dear Reader,

The authors, who are good friends of mine, asked me to write a little something about my experiences as a vegetarian. Let's make that a vegetarian who eats fish. Anyway, they felt I might have some "advice" or some helpful bits of information to pass along to you.

It's true that I've had experiences with different kinds of food. It must be eight years ago that I chucked all my junk food, meat, sugar, alcohol, and mother's cooking to go the way of culinary purity. I taught myself how to cook natural foods, how to substitute for flesh, sugar, and white flour, how to cure many illnesses without medicines, and how to get along on less.

What got me motivated? One fact that struck me then was our gluttony. We are a nation of gluttons. That's pigs, you know! Most of our grain goes to feed beef cattle. That same grain, distributed to hungry humans, could be feeding eight times the number that slaughtered cattle does. And you know which country consumes the most meat, don't you?

Another thing; I couldn't stand to put those emulsifiers, carcinogens, preservatives, coloring agents, bleaching agents, etc. into my gut any longer. I've read enough books and studies to convince me that the accepted "experts" don't know enough about what the commericial interests are offering us to eat. Trust the government to determine what's best for my body? No thanks! USDA "choice" means nothing to me. It's just a stamp on the side of a dead animal. The FDA has had numbers of food additives on their GRAS (Generally Recognized As Safe) list for years and later found evidence to the contrary. My safety isn't on their list apparently.

The whole food business — and if food isn't BIG business, I don't know what is — scared me. I studied for nearly a year to learn all I could about nutrition beyond the oversimplified four-food-group routine that doctors get quizzed on in med school. And there's plenty out there to learn about. Even though they may not be recognized by medical practitioners, many people have spent lifetimes studying the nutritional values of foods. Then there are the reports on problems of food additives and the real dangers of overconsumption of meat. There are the concepts of fasting, food combining, herbology, juice therapies, holistic health, organic gardening, lowering stress levels, and so on and on. Sometimes I am amazed by the things that have opened up to me as a result of my giant step away from junking out.

Why did I fall back into it? Why make the effort to become an expert organic food non-flesh eater, then go back to being a carnivorous junkster once again? Beats me. It seemed like the thing to do at the time. Probably because I had gone too far in one direction — too much of a good thing. I had no real complaints about my style, other than the difficulty in finding restaurants to cater to my specialized needs. But we are all individuals, you know, and I found myself with some individual pressures and some dramatic changes in my routine. I changed a little as a result. My diet went with me.

You could say I tested my theory that non-meat, pure food eating would make me healthier, wealthier and wiser. I tested by eating the way the majority of Americans do — hamburgers, ice cream sundaes, liquor, pie, coffee, more coffee, french fries, blueberry-turnovers, steak, ham, chocolate chip cookies, and anything else that wasn't moving. I pigged out. It was truly a case of going from one extreme to another.

How did the test turn out? I was right. For me, eating a basically natural food vegetarian diet is best. Oh, don't get me wrong. I didn't suffer a lot while I was back on junk. No stomach pains, indigestion, constipation (except after eating steak or prime rib), diarrhea, or pimples. Of course I did manage to put on 15 pounds in the 18 months of my spree. But who's counting calories when all those goodies are so conveniently located along the city streets; donuts here, tacos across the way, and fried chicken up the block? I'd forgotten how easy it was when you're hooked on taste, convenience and free enterprise sales tactics.

Eventually I had to admit to the results of my experiment. I was getting fat and I could not continue to push aside the knowledge about what I was consuming. I made the decision to clean up my eating act and fasted for ten days. This gave me the impetus to put my taste buds under control once again and to eat much more sensibly. I'm not a true vegetarian now. And I don't know if I will be again. I eat fish once or twice per week. I feel better having it as an option in my diet. But in general I try to consume only fresh vegetables and fruits (organically grown whenever possible), and to obtain protein from things like tofu, brewer's yeast, beans, grains, seeds, and occasionally milk products. This is good for me — for now.

While I'm writing this I'm drinking a beer and eating some peanuts — hardly the habits of a "health nut", right? For that matter, I'll still eat a piece of pie here or there and I love the taste and buzz of coffee. But I do try to moderate these "vices" so they don't become habits. I really do want to live a long life, free from debilitating health problems and guilt over having to always kill animals to receive nourishment. There is a good way to live for me, and for the time being I think I've found it.

If you are looking for ways to get your eating act together a little better, I'd like to make a few suggestions:

★ Digest the material you've read in this book. Read some of the recommended works for further information. The more you learn and understand, the easier it will be for you to leave the old habits and the harder it will be to eat without considering the consequences.

★ Substitute new foods for old slowly. Let the taste develop. Don't force it.

★ Eliminate sugar (straight and in processed foods) and use honey, maple syrup or date sugar instead. Limit the use of those items however. All are concentrated sugars.

★ Add brewer's yeast (nutritional yeast) to your diet. It's really a wonder food. The taste is repulsive at the beginning, but a couple of spoonfuls in tomato juice might be a good way to start. I drink 2 tablespoons dissolved in water every day and extra doses for hangovers, depression, listlessness, falling hair, cracked nails, and canker sores! It's my elixir.

* Read labels.

* Don't trust sweet-sounding, sexy-looking people on TV commercials who try to sell you food or drink to add life and energy to your day.

* Eat more raw foods. Some experts say 75% of our diet should be raw fruits and vegetables. Do what you can to add more of these life-giving substances to your diet.

* Substitute whole grains and whole grain flours for white rice and white flour.

* Try herb teas or grain beverages in place of your usual coffee or pekoe.

* Try to get certified raw milk and raw milk products instead of pasteurized or homogenized ones. Buying from a certified dairy like Alta-Dena in California will eliminate the fear of contracting milk-borne diseases like Salmonella and the raw milk is much better for you than the cooked product — if you are a milk-tolerant person. (Some people aren't.)

* Take it slow and don't give up. If you backslide a little, that's OK. Just set new goals and try again. I did backflips down Everest for 18 months before I put on the brakes. Remember the key: What's right for you is known only by you.

Finally, use any or all or none of the above suggestions. I'm happy with what I do, and I expect you'll be happy with your decisions. However, if you'd like some help finding answers to any questions this book has raised or that you've formulated as a result of trying this new life, write to me in *care of the publisher. I promise to reply to your queries to the best of my ability/experiences as a concerned and well-informed eater. I also have lots of friends who have been down the natural food-vegetarian path for quite a long time. We'd all be glad to help someone who's getting "smart."*

My best to you all,

Ernest

BOOKS TO READ

PRIMERS

Acciardo, Marcia, *Light Eating for Survival*. Wethersfield, Conn: Omango D'Press, 1977.

Gay, Kathlyn, Martin & Marla, *Get Hooked on Vegetables*. New York: Julian Messner div. Simon & Schuster, 1978.

Goeltz, J. & Lazenby, P., *Thanks, I Needed That, Beginner's Natural Food Cookbook*. Salt Lake City, Utah: Hawkes Publishing Inc., 1975.

Hunter, Beatrice Trum, *Natural Foods Primer*. New York: Simon and Schuster, Inc., 1972.

Kolson, Carol and Stan, *Holistic H.E.L.P. Handbook*. Phoenix: International Holistic Center, 1979.

Robertson, Laurel, et al., *Laurel's Kitchen*. Berkeley, Ca.: Nilgiri Press, 1978.

COOKBOOKS

Acciardo, Marcia, *Light Eating for Survival*. Wethersfield, Conn.: Omango D'Press, 1977.

Brown, Edward E., *Tassajara Cooking*. Berkeley: Shambahala Publications, Inc., 1973.

Dinshah, Freda, *The Vegan Kitchen*. Malaga, N.J.: American Vegan Society, 1973.

Duquette, Susan, *Sunburst Farm Family Cookbook* (Second Edition). Santa Barbara, CA.: Woodbridge Press Publishing Company, 1978.

Ewald, Ellen, *Recipes for a Small Planet*. New York: Ballantine Books, 1973.

Ford, M.W., et al., *The Deaf Smith Country Cookbook*. New York: Macmillan Publishing Company, Inc., 1973.

Hagler, Louise (Ed.), *The Farm Vegetarian Cookbook*. (Revised Ediition). Summertown, Tennessee: The Book Publishing Company, 1978.

Heartsong, Toni and Bob, *The Heartsong Tofu Cookbook*. Miami: Banyan Books, 1978.

Hewitt, Jean, *The New York Times Natural Foods Cookbook*. New York: Avon Books, 1971.

Hooker, Alan, *Vegetarian Gourmet Cookery.* San Francisco: 101 Productions, 1978.

Hurd, Rosalie and Frank, *Ten Talents.* Chisholm, Minn., Dr. & Mrs. Frank J. Hurd, 1968.

Kulvinskas, Viktoras, *Love Your Body.* Wethersfield, Conn.: Omango D'Press, 1976.

Landgrebe, Gary, *Tofu Goes West.* Palo Alto, CA.: Fresh Press, 1979.

Lappe, Francis Moore, *Diet for a Small Planet.* New York: Ballantine Books, 1973.

Robertson, Laurel, et al., *Laurel's Kitchen.* Berkeley, CA.: Nilgiri Press, 1976.

Shurtleff, William and Akiko Aoyagi, *The Book of Tofu* (Revised Edition). New York: Ballantine Books, 1979.

Thomas, Anna, *Vegetarian Epicure.* (Book 1). New York: Vintage Books, 1972.

Thomas, Anna, *Vegetarian Epicure* (Book 2). New York: Alfred A. Knopf, 1972.

Walker, Dr. Norman, *Vegetarian Guide to Diet and Salad.* Phoenix: Norwalk Press Publishers, 1970.

HEALTH

Airola, Paavo, *Are You Confused?* Phoenix: Health Plus Publishers, 1979.

Airola, Paavo, *How to Eat Well.* Phoenix: Health Plus Publishers, 1974.

Bragg, Paul and Patricia, *Toxicless Diet and Body Purification.* Santa Barbara, CA.: Health Science, 1979.

Clark, Linda, *Stay Young Longer.* New York: Pyramid Books, 1971.

Deal, Sheldon, *New Life Through Nutrition.* Tucson: New Life Publishing, 1974.

Donsbach, Kurt, *Nutritional Approach to Superhealth.* Huntington Beach, CA.: International Institute of Natural Health Sciences, Inc., 1980.

Jackson and Teague, *The Handbook of Alternatives to Chemical Medicine.* Oakland, CA.: Lawton-Teague Publications, 1975.

Jensen, Bernard, *Vital Foods for Total Health.* Solona Beach, CA.: Bernard Jensen Products, 1971.

Kulvinska, Viktoras, *Survival into the 21st Century.* Wethersfield, Conn.: Omango D'Press, 1975.

Malstrom, Stan, *Own Your Own Body.* Orem, Utah: Fresh Mountain Air, 1977.

FOOD COMBINING

Callela, John R., *Cooking Naturally.* Berkeley, CA.: And/Or Press, 1978.

Hurd, Frank and Rosalie, *Ten Talents.* Chisholm, Minn., Dr. & Mrs. Frank J. Hurd, 1968.

Lappe, Francis Moore, *Diet for a Small Planet.* New York: Ballantine Books, 1973.

Null, Gary and staff, *Food Combining Handbook.* New York: Jove Publications, 1980.

Shelton, Herbert, *Food Combining Made Easy.* San Antonio, Texas: Dr. Shelton's Health School, 1951.

WEIGHT/DIETING

Airola, Paavo, *How to Keep Slim, Healthy and Young With Juice Fasting.* Phoenix: Health Plus, 1980.

Donsbach, Kurt, *The Overweight Problem.* Huntington Beach, CA.: The International Institute of Natural Health Sciences, 1977.

Bragg, Paul and Patricia, *Natural Way to Reduce.* Santa Barbara, CA.: Health Science, (no date).

Birkinshaw, Elsye, *Think Slim, Be Slim.* Santa Barbara, CA.: Woodbridge Press Publishing Co., 1976.

Burroughs, Stanley, *The Master Cleanser.* Kailua, Hawaii: Stanley Burroughs, 1976.

Orbach, Susie, *Fat is a Feminist Issue.* New York: Berkeley Publishing Corp., 1980.

Partee, Phillip, *Layman's Guide to Fasting and Losing Weight.* Sarasota, FL.: Sprout Publications, Inc., 1979.

FASTING

Airola, Paavo, *How to Keep Slim, Healthy and Young with Juice Fasting.* Phoenix: Health Plus Publications, 1980.

Bragg, Paul and Patricia, *Miracle of Fasting.* Santa Barbara, CA.: Health Science, 1979.

Burroughs, Stanley, *Healing for the Age of Enlightenment.* Kailua, Hawaii: Stanley Burroughs, 1976.

Burroughs, Stanley, *The Master Cleanser.* Kailua, Hawaii: Stanley Burroughs, 1976.

Christopher, John, *Dr. Christopher's 3-Day Cleansing Program.* Provo, Utah: Christopher Publications, (no date).

Cott, Allan et al., *Fasting as a Way of Life.* New York: Bantam Books, 1977.

Ehret, Arnold, *Rational Fasting.* Beaumont, CA.: Ehret Literature Publishing Co., 1971.

Shelton, Herbert, *Fasting Can Save Your Life.* Chicago: Natural Hygiene Press, 1967.

Szekely, Edmond B., *Essene Gospel of Peace No. 1.* San Diego: Academy Books, 1975.

Walker, Norman, *Raw Fruit and Vegetable Juices.* Phoenix: Norwalk Press, 1936.

ETHICAL VEGETARIANISM

Altman, Nathaniel, *Eating for Life.* Wheaton, Ill.: Theosophical Publishing House, 1973.

Barkas, Janet, *The Vegetable Passion.* New York: Charles Scribner's Sons, 1975.

Holmer-Gore, V.A., *These We Have Not Loved.* Essex, England: C.W. Daniel Co., 1971

Holzer, Hans, *Vegetarian Way of Life.* New York: Pyramid Books 1973.

L'Amour, Rose, *Who Cares for Animals?* Santa Fe Springs, CA.: Stockton Trade Press, Inc., 1971.

Parham, Barbara, *What's Wrong With Eating Meat?* Denver: Ananda Marga Publications, 1980.

Scharffenberg, John A., *Problems With Meat.* Santa Barbara, CA.: Woodbridge Press Publishing Co., 1979.

Szekely, Edmond B., *Essene Gospel of Peace No. 1.* San Diego: Academy Books, 1975.

ADDITIVES, PESTICIDES, ETC.

Carson, Rachel, *Silent Spring*. Greenwich, Conn.: Fawcett Publications, 1973.

Hunter, Beatrice Trum, *Consumer Beware*. New York: Bantam Books, 1972.

Hunter, Beatrice Trum, *Food Additives and Your Health*. New Canaan, Conn.: Keats Publishing, 1971.

Jacobson, Michael, *Eater's Digest: Consumer's Factbook of Food Additives*. Garden City, N.J.: Doubleday and Co., 1972.

Marine, G. and Van Allen, J., *Food Pollution*. New York: Holt, Rinehart and Winston, 1973.

Turner, James, *The Nader Report: The Chemical Feast*. New York: Grossman Publishers, 1970.

Verret, Jacqueline, *Eating May Be Hazardous to Your Health*. New York: Simon and Schuster, 1974.

Winter, Ruth, *Beware of the Food You Eat*. New York: Signet Books, 1971.

Winter, Ruth, *Consumer's Dictionary of Food Additives*. New York: Crown Publishers, Inc., 1972.

Winter, Ruth, *Poisons in Your Food*. New York: Crown Publications, Inc., 1971.